The Grace of God

The Grace of God

Robert P. Radloff

THE GRACE OF GOD

By Robert P. Radloff

ISBN # 1-897373-22-8

Printed by Word Alive Press
131 Cordite Road, Winnipeg, MB R3W 1S1
www.wordalivepress.ca

—Table of Contents

1: The Road Often Travelled

CHILDHOOD MEMORIES ON THE Saskatchewan prairies involve the most elemental senses.

The sun touching our faces on a late February's day as we play on the south side of the house, the side where the sun's rays briefly gather fleeting strength, warm the earth by the stuccoed wall and, for a short time, liberate it from winter frost. The sun warms our faces as if to reward us for our foray from the house. It warms the good earth for an afternoon, allowing the soil to release its wholesome smell.

The hollow sound of our snow boots crunching over crisp snowdrifts, their surface hardened by the winter gusts and relentless cold. The drifts form arching mounds that partially bury the twisted barbed wire fences and willow bushes, once a formidable barrier to little adventurers. We pass over these barriers easily now, our snowsuits swishing as we confidently walk the solid white dunes. The wire and willow tops poke from their wintry prison here and there, clutching at our snow boots as we pass over them now. As best they can, they clutch at us as if to remind us they will return.

The plaintive cry of the killdeer in the hot summer, scurrying across the dry grass with a faked broken wing. She runs a confused route, wanting to draw our attention to her feigned plight, wanting to draw us away from her nest crowded with mottled eggs. We are wise to her scheme. But we remember our mother's warning: "They'll put out your eyes if you get too close, you know." We watch the act in the shimmering heat waves without moving.

A late-September moon looming through a fall evening over fields of grain being harvested at midnight by a fleet of combines, their headlights bobbing and shuddering in the distance as the hulking equipment jostles over the land. The light of the moon is so bright as to render headlights unnecessary. A hint of frost touches our skin and chills us as we stand beside the now cold pickup truck—the metal skin, once warmed by the autumn sun, now adds to the cold tableau.

But the clearest memory of all is the wind. It's always there: loud and blustery, frenzied, whipping through winter's darkness, tearing at our winter coats, latches, shutters, and appendages, biting furiously at exposed skin; twisting vehicle exhausts in crazy wisps on a frigid evening on a darkened town street in front of the curling rink; or softly moaning, ever rising and subsiding, on a hot summer's afternoon, pushing the growing crops as waves on the endless horizon. Wind is the heart of this place—kind and knowing, unforgiving and cruel.

The wind carries many memories from its travels through this lonesome land. It shares these with us when we listen to it, even after many years have passed—even when we are assured that these were erased, or so we thought, by years of business and the din of life.

Even stray crosswinds carry us back to specific places…

*****

A sudden gust strikes the car, causing it to shudder.

"Is he coming back?" I asked.

My voice seemed loud breaking the long silence after my father left the car. I hadn't wanted to attract attention; I had learned life was easier when you didn't. It seemed like the words were much bolder than intended, perhaps because normally no one spoke much in these situations, especially not the kids.

Still, I needed an answer, and, always the troublemaker, I persisted.

"When will he be back?"

The wind this time brushed gently against the side of the car, causing it to rock, ever so slightly, as I waited for a response.

"Your father will be back soon enough," was the answer.

Of course. That was always the answer. I guess I knew that. People often ask questions they know the answer to, just to hear the answer they believe to be true.

I peered out the front window of the car. My father's figure grew more and more contorted in the shimmering heat waves as he continued to walk down the gravel road in front of us. His briskly striding figure became small as he followed the long row of power poles paralleling the gravel road; finally, it disappeared over a slight rise in the horizon. To our left and right were endless fields of summer wheat, bowing and rising as waves in the sea. No fences—just endless crop dissected by gravel roads like the one we now sat on. The odd farmhouse dotted the landscape, each complete with a collection of wind-bruised trees and low carriganaugh bushes wrapped around them for shelter from the wind. Behind us, like before us, stretched an endless gravel road, shimmering in the summer heat as it rose and fell with the gentle landscape.

We settled in, and the hours began to pass, slowly, tediously. My entire family, except my father of course, were sitting, sleeping, playing at various stations in the car at the side of the road halfway between our home in Prince Albert, and Star City, Saskatchewan, where my father's parents lived. Each of us went to our respective stations in the vehicle as if on cue during these events. This wasn't new to us. We had often been loaded into the car and driven part way to a lot of places; part way because all too often Dad was perplexed about whether to go or not. Halfway there invariably would find us parked by the side of the road while Dad sorted things out, not knowing whether to continue or return home.

It could have been worse. More often than not a trip could entail driving halfway to our destination, turning around and driving back two miles (yes, we had miles in those days) and then careening to a screaming halt—screaming car, screaming kids—turning a wild doughnut in the middle of the road and heading back in the original direction. Often he'd do this multiple times, gaining speed with each new direction taken, sometimes reaching speeds of 90 miles an hour on the gravel backroads until he'd feel right about which way we were going.

So we were thankful for small mercies. Not that we'd let our guard down. Any trip could easily escalate into one of those. And then, of course, it could involve the unthinkable fury of short but brutal physical assaults on the rest of us for our alleged contribution to this dilemma. Our contribution was, of course, that we were there.

Hours slipped by. I traced the slow progress of the sun as it pushed the shadow of the doorpost across the back seat and onto the floor. Time passed slowly. Meanwhile, the wind gently, then vigorously, rocked the car and its contents, desperately seeking to play. No luck. We had no time for that, and besides, we were not allowed outside. We kept busy carving patterns in the new carpet on the floor in advance of the progressing doorpost shadow. With careful planning the two alignments would be perfectly parallel when they met. Anything to keep our interest. Outside, moaning in its rising and falling crescendos, the wind continued rocking the car. This, in combination with the warm sun, put most of the kids to sleep. Sprawled out in the back of the White Rambler Classic 660 station wagon and propped up against the back door, they sleep at their posts.

We'd travelled this road many times before, but had only made it to my grandparents' home once that I could remember in my lifetime. They were the "bad people"—at least that was what I had heard. That's what Dad said and of course he was always right.

"You have to let the dead bury the dead," he'd say, dead meaning spiritually dead, of course. You had to look for the spiritual meaning in these things. "They are of the world, so the world can love them," he'd add. And being students of the Word ourselves we knew that "of the world" meant they were not righteous. That didn't need to be said. It was the world according to Dad.

Without warning, Dad had returned. Like a fool I'd fallen asleep—I'd let my guard down, lulled by the warmth of the late afternoon sun on the warm vinyl seats pressed against my cheek. The door opened, letting in the previously muffled outside sounds for a brief moment. It closed with a loud thud that immediately startled the rest of the kids awake into attention and silent wariness. Dad's face was red and drawn from the strenuous walk, and his cheek twitched with suppressed emotion. The unpredictable, volatile presence had returned to our world. We braced for his next move, hoping he would start the car and return us to the safety of home.

Then suddenly it began, an angry tirade of uninterrupted verbal abuse, growing louder against the faint protests of our mother. Inevitably words were no longer enough, and he gave vent to his anger on our mother's body with quick punches and more shouts. The kids, now huddled in terror in the back seat, would react to each sickening blow with a chorus of cries, as if we ourselves were being beaten. Then suddenly, like a prairie thunderstorm, the fearful wave of anger subsided. No more blows. Only the faint crying of mom, the muffled sobs of the kids, and the uncaring hiss of the wind outside the car in the aftermath. My dad, flushed with anger but satisfied that we all shared his pain, started up the motor and slowly turned the car around, its wheels crunching on the gravel the only sound to be heard. We were going home.

This part was fairly standard, with a few slight variations from week to week. You didn't dare think it was over for the day, however, not even when you actually reached the house, especially not 10 minutes after a tirade. You wouldn't hope it was over, lest your hope be known and subsequently dashed with the terrible slowing of the car. If the car slowed then you knew there would be more violence. Sometimes vented once again on mom, or if the gods determined, on one of us kids riding in the back who had the audacity to cry a little too loudly. Once home we retreated quickly to the relative safety of our rooms, hoping there had been enough violence and uncertainty for one day.

*****

If only my earliest memories held the smells and sounds of the prairies. If only my past was dominated by the wind. But that wasn't to be. My world was dominated by "Dad," who ruled our family like the wrathful demi-god of a small island in a sea of never-ending grass. His whims were to be obeyed and his rages felt by all of us, but most of all by our mother.

So welcome to my hell in 1966. A hell dominated by punishment and fear, and worst of all, by never knowing if or when it might ever end.

2: Beginnings

DAD WAS THE YOUNGEST in a family of six siblings and the son of Frank Radloff, a businessman in the Carrot River Valley in northern Saskatchewan. Frank was the owner of several Serve U stores, farmland, and other assorted portions of real estate. He was successful by anyone's standards and certainly by those of Saskatchewan 20 years after the Great Depression. He was known for being a tireless worker, strong as an ox and determined as a mule. He was reputed to be the strongest man in the Carrot River Valley, and in support of this title he would occasionally be seen carrying a 25-gallon drum of vinegar, pickles or other such liquid from the delivery bay behind the Serve U store to the front retail area.

Frank was a quiet man and an excellent father, and though he was known for his strength, he was highly intelligent as well. This combination, matched up early on with money from his wife, Alice, made for the early and sustained success of the family. They had both arrived in the area in 1905 from Nebraska. Frank and his father Frank Sr. started out on a small farm due south of Melfort. Young Frank would walk 10 miles each way to Melfort every day, where he worked for a local store owner learning the retail business. He wasn't much like his father, who was evidently a bit more used to being well to do than most in the area, and as a result they didn't get on well.

Soon Frank was looking for a place of his own in Star City, where he met Alice, who was up with her sisters for a short time to feed and care for her brothers, the Henning boys, who were working their father's farm. She was shy and retiring herself and got on well with Frank. Most were surprised to see they had so many children—seven in all—so quickly given it was reported Alice wasn't able to have children. While she retained some of the trappings of her mothers Jehovah's Witness faith, Frank's only genuine nod to religion was to bow deeply at the altar of hard work; his firm faith lay in the tangible salvation of steady toil. But, despite his hard ways and hard looks, he was at his core a gentle, soft-spoken man. The Radloff family flourished around his incredible capacity for work and ability to provide.

And so my father was raised with the values of church and toil under the hard eyes and silent looks of a local legend. Perhaps this was the role for a youngest son, the baby of the family, but he made the most of it. He grew up spoiled and pampered as only the youngest son of a self-made man can. He was brilliant like many of the Radloff kids. His brother Glenn finished Grade 12 by 14. Paul Rae wasn't much different except that he was hard to handle from day one, certainly too much for his mother, and his father was too preoccupied with business to take the time to straighten things out. As if that was humanly possible.

Paul Rae was always the life of the party, brilliant at putting on plays, entertaining and dealing with people in the store. This latter quality made up only partly for the high maintenance and undesirable high profile he created for his father. Ultimately they arrived at an accommodation that seemed to work for both. Dad took care of the dry goods upstairs in the store. Grandpa took care of the produce downstairs. There was a lot more distance between the two than 10 vertical feet between floors.

However, as my father approached adulthood, three major changes severed his relationship with his father for good: he got married, he found religion, and, acting on his newfound faith, he chose a vocation and school, of which his father disapproved. Against the threats and protests of his father, my dad decided to attend Bible School.

——3: The First Car

MANY OF US REMEMBER PERIODS of our lives by certain milestones or symbols of that period. For some it is the music of the period. For others it may be the start of a vocation, a relocation to another country or a war fought in or returned from.

For me it is cars. Fitting enough, as it seemed we spent most of our lives in them.

Perhaps it was his own father's disapproval and unbending will that caused my father's rage and indecision on our weekly drives. Perhaps it was because his original decision to go to Pentecostal Bible School had been watered down by a decision to go to United Church theological seminary in Saskatoon and pastor nearby United Churches, this to provide money to pay for his growing family—evidently not an option available to Dad in the Pentecostal system. Whatever the cause, their war came to an abrupt climax one sunny summer morning in our shiny, two-toned green '56 Dodge.

*****

It was only 10 a.m. and the summer sun had already warmed the prairie landscape, a beautiful morning with all the promise of a greater afternoon to come.

The Dodge was a gift from his father, a fact that certainly disturbed my dad's theory that his father never did anything to assist him in his days of bible school. It may have been the closest my grandfather, an unyielding man, could ever come to a compromise. I remember it through my four-year-old eyes as a beauty—long, beautiful, two-tone green and shiny with big comfortable seats. It had a cord strategically placed on the back of the front seat for back-seat residents like me to hang on to, a hard-pressed metal dash and fabric seats, an automatic transmission and a radio with big shiny knobs too. In those days, that was pretty close to all the options.

We had already spent a good hour that morning careening up and down the access road to Star City and that cord behind the front seat was coming in very handy. Dad couldn't make up his mind, and each change of perspective resulted in another foray down the gravel—each time with more and more speed. Toward Star City, then away from Star City, back and forth as the battle raged in our father's mind and on the gear shift. Unfortunately for our nice new Dodge, on the last of these high speed races—this time headed towards Star City—Dad, suddenly filled with frustration and indecision, shrieked at the top of his lungs, punched the gas pedal to the mat and pointed the beautiful, two-toned, every-option Dodge towards a large black poplar tree beside the Royalite gas station. The seconds before impact, Dad screaming and kids crying while we closed in on the big old tree, were moments to remember. Time moves slowly just before such momentous collisions, I'm not sure why. You have time to wonder why this is happening; why the gas station is closed this morning; what the neighbourhood is going to think; will the car get over that ditch between you and the tree?

And then the collision.

The impact was deafening. I was in the back seat where the sound of crunching metal and breaking glass filled the air, mixed with screams from the family and dust from the seats. Then, suddenly, stunned silence. The world was temporarily removed from our senses. As the scene sank in, the world came back in jolted perspective. Bailing out of the right rear door, I stood next to the mangled wreck.

Miraculously, no one was seriously hurt, well, except the beautiful two-toned green Dodge. It gurgled and clucked as the motor block slowly cooled. I remember looking up at the gas station. The tall gas pumps, their clear glass heads full of purple gasoline and pump handles motionless at their sides, looked on at the crippled vehicle's demise. They didn't appear to understand either.

As the dust settled, my father's rage over his own indecision precipitated my first meeting with my grandfather.

*****

He was an imposing figure, true to the rumours. At four or five, I was more than a little apprehensive of this stocky, silent sentinel, and yet all my memories of his actions were that of a silent kindness. Firm, silent, maybe even scary, but decisive, practical and kind. He stood for hours with me picking the carefully cultured peas in his big garden for grandma's evening meal, motioning mostly to the next row as we worked our way down the pea patch, not speaking. He communicated by gestures and grimaces on his wide, strong-featured face. He worked silently and tirelessly and so did I. You were afraid not to, really, yet it was in his nature to do so and in mine. We were a pair.

A brief call from the house would end our work adventure. We'd return to the house to the pragmatic praise of my grandmother, who took the fruits of our work and began the chore of shucking the peas with my cousin Janice. The hulk and I parted without words, both attesting to each others' strength. The object of his exercise realized, he returned to the depths of his study. It's a good man who takes the time to test the mettle of little visitors, I think.

4: Isolation

FROM THAT TIME ONWARD, my father began to isolate his growing family. At the time of the crash of the Dodge there were four of us kids: Mark, my oldest brother, Doug, myself, and Rhonda. Later, Brock, Paul, and Chris would arrive, but only the older four of us really remember how it was at the beginning.

After the crash we stopped the weekly insanity of our drives to Star City. These were replaced with insane drives to other places. We saw many of the good clay roads of Saskatchewan by these means. Fields of wheat, endless in expanse and bowing to the passing wind, was a common element to these trips, as was the endless wait for dad to return from his walks. We never went to see my grandparents again and my grandparents never came to see us.

This signalled the beginning of our gypsy years. Before I graduated from high school we would live in Tessier, Delisle, Leask, Canwood, Prince Albert, Hinton, Seba Beach, Calgary, Edmonton, Vilna, Smoky Lake, and eventually, Vancouver. You get to know a lot of kids in school this way, but not for long. For obvious reasons I grew to hate being "the new kid" every year.

5: Tessier and Delisle—the Second Car

TESSIER, SASKATCHEWAN, WAS OUR FIRST STOP. Dad was the pastor for the United Church, his first real test in the ministry. This was a small church, not out of keeping with the town itself, which was a small town even for Saskatchewan standards. In Saskatchewan you could pretty much predict the size of the town by the number of grain elevators in it. Fittingly, Tessier had just one, and one café, one general store and one school. You get the picture: a town of not more than 200 people at that time; less today.

Even in the late Fifties, this town, with the smaller farms in the vicinity, was pretty much dead quiet. Better roads and vehicles allowed farm workers and farmers to go further afield for goods and services. Still, old ideas die hard, and Tessier was no exception. A small number of faithful attended the small white church kitty-corner to the two-storey white manse where we lived. It was 1959 when Mark, Doug, Rhonda and I posed in our snowsuits in front of the house, the snow salting the bushes that circled the front yard behind us.

We were there a year and a half before Dad was called to pastor in Delisle, 10 kilometres up the road from Tessier toward Saskatoon. It was pretty much the big time: Delisle had three elevators and lots of people, around 700. A veritable metropolis with a hospital and everything, it was just the perfect setting for an aspiring pastor and his aspiring juvenile delinquent son. Dad was really busy with the church and pretty successful in inspiring new life into the already large congregation. He was rewarded for those efforts by having two additional works added to his responsibilities: Islandia and Donovan. During this time he was also commuting to the University of Saskatchewan in Saskatoon where he was completing his Bachelor of Arts and Diploma in Theology. Needless to say, his attention was focused away from us and on his new works. A perfect opportunity.

With Dad safely distracted and relatively happy with his growing successful ministry, I must have realized it was all up to me provide chaotic continuity. By the time I was six I was responsible for burning down the garage at the church manse, destroying a new house under construction, letting the air out of most of the tires of the farm implements at the local dealership, destroying my brothers' tree house, bringing my mother's china cabinet crashing to the dining room floor, burning my father's seminary books and driving our elderly babysitter to the brink of insanity. Doug and I were frequent participants in dirt lump and rock fights with the town's other kids. We even managed to hitchhike 25 kilometres to the Scout camp where we engaged in mortal combat with porcupines and destroyed more construction works, taking our terror campaign further afield. I would often spend a quiet summer afternoon with a friend on the manse veranda roof throwing sticks and mud mixed with curses at various passers-by. A pastor's kid gone wild, I suppose. Well, I had help—I was given to understand my friends were a bad influence on me. I wasn't really that bad. The Oviet twins and Gordy Carlseneous—they all contributed to the problem, not to mention my older brother Doug.

It was perhaps for all those reasons it was decided one day that I should accompany my father and a church elder to the nearby community of Canwood to attend a church service, as opposed to staying at home and "entertaining" myself. The time and date were set. Given we would be using the back roads, it was determined that we would use a pickup loaned for this event. I remember it well: a brown 1960 International Harvester pick-up, or "corn binder" truck as they were affectionately called. They were never built for speed or comfort. There I sat, firmly ensconced between two pillars of the church, lurching from one bump to bump, pothole to pothole, the tires splashing up the recently deposited rain from every rut. Jarred and jostled, we continued interminably toward our objective. Perhaps this was the hell they kept talking about.

After some hours we arrived and the resolute brown buckboard disgorged its unwilling 6-year-old passenger on the steps of the little white Pentecostal church and we went inside.

There was something different about this place. The building was the same shape as ours, just smaller. Same hardwood pews, same ornate pulpit where, no doubt, someone would speak for endless hours, and the same arched windows. But something was different and I couldn't put my finger on it. Soon the church was packed, each arrival greeting the others already gathered with a hearty smile, a handshake, and a "Praise the Lord" or "God is good." The song service began and the songs were sung with great enthusiasm mixed with the occasional "Halleluiah" or "Thank you Jesus." I strained from my back row seat to see the proceedings. Suddenly the singing ended. The congregation seated itself with a mighty creaking of the pews and rustle of clothing, and the clunking of songbooks in their receptacles. A quiet descended over the crowd as the preacher, an intense and earnest man, stood up to speak after a polite introduction. He spoke about Jesus and how He died for our sins. He told how there is only one sacrifice acceptable to God and how this Jesus, the Son of God, made that sacrifice for me so I could come to know God and have a new life in Him. He spoke about how we could all have this new life in God by simply accepting this sacrifice and accepting Jesus into our hearts as the way to God.

Though he spoke to the hundreds there, I knew he was speaking right to me. I had no doubt. He asked how many would like to accept Jesus into their hearts: "Just put up your hand." I knew I wanted that more than anything else in my life and I put up my hand. It was almost like everything else in life was on hold at that moment. As was the congregation's custom, all the members went to the prayer room after the service. Because I had put up my hand I was invited, too. As I began to pray a simple prayer in that packed little room, a tremendous peace came over me. And God, the active force of the universe, met me at the centre of my being. Nothing would be the same again.

As I rode home that night I don't recall a single bump or lurch from the little brown truck all the way home. I'm sure the potholes hadn't left; however, it was like I had an air cushioned ride—I remember that distinctly. I was pretty sure that was going to be normal from now on, but unfortunately, I was wrong.

*****

Two things occurred later that year that were to dramatically change our lives: the first was that my father refused to accept his ordination in the United Church, the second was that my father resigned from his ministry in the United Church and began a career in teaching. Following closely on the heels of these decisions, we left Delisle for Leask, Saskatchewan, my father's new teaching assignment.

Oh, right! About that second car. We had acquired a 1960 Ford Falcon to replace the Dodge. It could best be described as basic transportation. It was robin's-egg blue with four doors and bench seats, a slant-six powerplant and "three-on–the-tree" column manual shift, pressed metal dashboard, vinyl interior and rubber flooring. The fake pearl handle top on the end of the shifter was the one deference to luxury afforded by the factory. But despite its humble appearance, it was to prove its mettle at high speeds on many a backcountry road, driven mercilessly by its new owner.

Between Deslisle and Leask we headed for the respite of Bell Butte, Saskatchewan. This proved to be a spiritual renewal for our father in the summer of 62, a haven from his heart-wrenching decision to refuse the ordination of the United Church. There he was able to rest for a time in a restorative ministry of the Shalums and the local Mennonite Brethren church.

6: Leask

LEASK WAS OUR FIRST EXPERIENCE as normal members of a local community; our parents no longer pastors and we no longer pastor's kids—PKs. You might say the pressure was off. You can't appreciate exactly what this means if you have never been a pastor or a PK. Suffice it to say a pastor is necessarily under considerably more scrutiny than pretty much any professional to be found in a small rural town in Saskatchewan. Pastors were, of a consequence, under significant pressure to be "nice." PKs like myself, however, were under equal pressure from our peers to be "not nice," a role I had filled with accolades up until now. This, and the fact that I had a real and impacting experience with God prior to our move to Leask, served to temper my previously legendary bad behaviour.

Things were going to be normal now. Dad taught school, my mother substituted and we attended the local Pentecostal Church. No doubt the presence of this church in the community had something to do with Dad choosing to live in Leask. Dad had decided that the Pentecostal Church was leading-edge on biblical doctrine, far in advance of the United Church. His expectations of the benefits associated with our attendance there were rather high. Initially some of these benefits were realized. Unfortunately, one of the benefits I believe my father envisioned was being involved in the ministry. And this did not occur primarily because the "PAOC," as they were often referred to around our house, did not recognize Dad's credentials from the United

Church, preferring that Dad attend a Pentecostal Bible College before he could be involved in Church ministry. It was an unhappy turn of events for all of us.

With the relief of "normalcy" still reverberating through the family's collective psyche, we began to enjoy the benefits of "normal" life that others around us were enjoying. That included upgrading of the household; out-houses gave way to in-house plumbing for us. This was a matter of mere curiosity for kids like myself but a matter of orders of magnitude regarding the reduction in workload for parents, Mom's in particular. This was followed shortly after by the introduction of an electric stove to replace the old wood-burning, iron- and nickel-plated monster previously employed. Our wood box days were suddenly over. Watching the orange glow of the element indicator light in the darkened kitchen was a fascination akin to watching the lunar landing.

Friends we made as kids were good in our small town. Friends our parents made with people in the church were tolerable if not stimulating. Despite this superficial ambiance, however, an undertow of dissatisfaction with the local pastor's abilities and understanding of scripture was beginning to make its presence felt. It was no doubt the consequence of "Master of Divinity meets the simplicity of PAOC doctrine" and PAOC leadership. All the understanding of Greek and Hebrew in the world could not undo the fact that lesser mortals were still in charge of the local church and did not wish to share position with non-conformists, no matter how well educated. And in that the dye was cast; we were to move to greener pastures. We were off to Canwood.

7: Canwood

CANWOOD WAS ANOTHER ONE-ELEVATOR TOWN, 80 km west of Prince Albert. For us it was another new school and the associated challenges of meeting and making new friends with the town kids, checking out the new house and getting into the appropriate part of the pecking order in the neighbourhood. For our father it was an entirely different task. He needed to teach to feed the family, but his choice of relocation to Canwood was no accident. He had previously enjoyed an association with the PAOC church as a United Church pastor in Canwood. He was determined to use this association to allow him to be more involved in the church at Canwood. His thought was to be involved in a lay pastor role to help the church reach its full potential. This was not to be for several reasons.

The first and most obvious reason was that my father was unwilling and, most would say, incapable of taking direction from church authority, since he was convinced that his interpretation of scripture was tantamount to infallible. No one understood the word like he did—or so he thought, forgetting, I suppose, that the Bible itself states that it is not subject to any private interpretation. This invariably led to disagreements with church leaders, and in father's case, to acts of verbal and even physical abuse of church leaders. I'm not sure where in the Scriptures it advocates a Christian Jihad. But for dad, he was justified even in these behaviours. I guess he hadn't read the fine print.

This inability to work within the established church was a source of frustration for my father—then and for many years to come. In turn, he was to take this frustration out on us—then, and for many years to come.

The second reason our participation in the local PAOC church was not to be was our brother Mark. Mark was the oldest. Mark was tall, dark and handsome. He did, however, suffer from big disabilities. At birth he received brain damage primarily from oxygen deprivation. As a result he had cerebral palsy, which worsened with time. Complications of this condition gave rise to epilepsy and some paralysis on his left side. He was frequently subject to grand-mal epileptic seizures. When Mark had a "spell" it was often dramatic, with physical contortions, frothing at the mouth and indiscernible groanings on his part. Unfortunately, some church leaders construed this condition as clear evidence of demonic possession. When it manifested itself during a church service and Sunday school we were directed to have Mark removed from the church—permanently. While my father was often the architect of his own confrontations, in this case, the decision to leave the church as a family was endorsed by all of us. We had learned over the years to live with Mark's condition and none of us shared our fellow churchgoers' terror of Mark's spiritual condition.

Actually, compared to the rest of us, we realized Mark was pretty much an angel. Mark was always a happy, bright young boy. Over time, however, the seizures took their toll. He dropped out of school and spent all his time at home. When we were younger we spent many hours playing tag with Mark at home. It was his favourite game. He'd tell us we were the chickens and he was the wolf. He was never as happy as when he was chasing us with his pronounced limp around the yard trying to catch us. Of course, he never could and really never wanted to. For him it was great fun.

Fortunately for Mark, he didn't realize he had been excommunicated from the church or why. The fallout for him, however, was both good and bad. Good, in that we had renewed some of our need to protect Mark. Suddenly, looking out for Mark was not the chore we had sometimes considered it to be. Bad, in that rejection from the church seemed to translate into rejection by the rest of the community as well.

To add to this, Dad began preaching in the school and to have loud shouting matches with other staff members. Doug was in Dad's class. His classmates turned on him and took every opportunity to humiliate and degrade him in revenge for his father's antics. It took on sordid proportions. His school life became a living hell. We weren't welcome on the streets in town.

Mark seemed to get many beatings from my father, probably related to the fact that he was seen as the source of the troubles. These beatings, however, were minor in comparison to those received by my mother at that time, likely for the same reason.

A natural consequence of our rejection from the community was that we began to have church in the home, and would travel far and wide during the summer to attend church camps where we were welcome. Another consequence was we began to befriend the native kids in our area, kids from the St. Dennis and Bird families who lived either on the neighbouring Sandy Lake reserve or on the outskirts of town. They had already been rejected by the mainstream community for many years. They turned out to be great friends, always ready for some fun adventure—sleeping out under the stars or having us into their homes where we could see real deer being skinned and cut on the kitchen floor. There was always something new. From them I learned the native stoic outlook. They could absorb incredible personal loss, insults and injustice and shrug it off with self-effacing humour. They shared everything with us, and we in turn with them. They were cultural survivors and helped us to be as well.

Church in the home offered my father a platform to drive home to all of us the sinfulness of the "world": how it was destined for judgment and how God would seek retribution on the nasty people who had rejected us. This sounded okay to me at the time. If a little fire and brimstone fell on our neighbours (except my native friends) it would have been just fine by me. It didn't happen, however. What did happen was that our family became introverted. With no contact with relatives, no contact with the real church and little contact with the community, we were our father's very own captive audiences—and the focus of his anger when things did not go well. Late nights were filled with the constant wild, reverberating sounds of domestic violence in the kitchen and living room next door.

About this time my father began to frequently reverse himself. It was a lot more than indecision. He would drive to one location and before arriving decide to return to our point of origin. Before arriving at our point of origin he would reverse himself and try to return to our original destination. This reversal could occur four or five times on a single journey. Each time a reversal occurred the speed of the vehicle would increase. The logical consequence of this would be that toward the end of the trip we could be hurtling down a dirt road at 90 miles per hour, kids crying, Dad hollering flushed and red in the face while raining blows as it served his fancy on my mother as the whole nightmare proceeded. Eventually it would end, of course, kids whimpering in the back while my mother confessed to being the cause of all the problems we ever had.

On one such adventure I recall becoming fed up with this method of travel, or more precisely, fed up with the intimidating effect it was designed to have on us. I recall on or about the third reversal, while we were doing approximately 70 miles an hour on the highway between Canwood and Shelbrook, SK. Given that the kids were not screaming loud enough in fear, my father decided to add weaving back and forth across the center line and narrowly missing oncoming traffic to the repertoire. And while the crescendo of the tumult in the vehicle heightened to his satisfaction I recall stating the unthinkable. It was a simple enough statement, not entirely unreasonable, but it was to have a chilling effect. I simply turned to the rest of the kids and said, "Don't cry, he just wants you to cry."

It seemed that time stood still for a brief moment while the impact of that statement sank into my siblings who, with one accord, began to cease crying; only the occasional whimper trailing off to silence. Looking up from my seat in the back I came face to face with the glare of my father in the rear-view mirror. I glared back. The car slowed and remained on our side of the centerline. A temporary reprieve had been won. There would be many more wild rides, but not today, and none that could evoke the requisite tears from me.

Temporary victories like this are akin to a captor backing down to the outrage of his captives when atrocities are pushed too far. They precipitate an uneasy truce between captor and captive, and last as long as the pent-up outrage of the captive outweighs the considered scheme of the captor. Timing in life is everything, and, of course, since the captor has ultimate control of the agenda and schedule, he can withdraw to press his advantage at another time of his choosing. In such circumstances it becomes imperative that the captive be ever watchful of the agenda, determining whether or not to press the fight button or the flight button. It's never easy being disempowered. Fear and suspicion become watchwords. Sleep doesn't come easy.

It is a particularly cruel mind shift when the captor and tormentor of a child is a parent figure. For the child, at some point the pain outweighs the supposed benefit of the social truce, or even the appearance of such a truce. At some point you cross the line and look to escape the confines of your prison camp experience by running away or dealing a fatal blow to your captor. For me it was the latter approach that gradually crept into consciousness.

With time, Canwood was to become a shadowy memory for all of us. It was where physical violence in the home became commonplace. It was where Doug correlated school with hell and received scars so deep in the process he still can't speak about them today. My recollections included hours of trying to sleep while screaming, hollering and beatings continued unabated, destroying furniture, trust and innocence. The need to act normal after the ritual was concluded added to the dichotomy experienced by my eight-year-old mind.

8: Prince Albert

THE FAMILY MOVED TO PRINCE ALBERT, an hour and a half drive east from Canwood and one of Saskatchewan's few real cities. For us, the change in scale was impressive. They had a bus system, a real downtown in the city core, expansive subdivision areas, multiple schools and endless alleys and streets to explore. And explore we did, to our hearts' content. Once firmly established in the city-kid pecking order, we used the friendships we developed there to expand our horizons of mayhem and fun. We also used these friendships to have reasons to stay away from home, a valuable enterprise since violence in the home had escalated in proportion to our new environs.

I returned to a reduced-scale terrorism, which consisted primarily of pranks like raiding backyard gardens and crabapple trees, throwing the proceeds of these raids at passing automobiles, primarily with numerous older neighbourhood kids my older brother Doug's age. It also included, however, breaking and entry into the local swimming pool concession to obtain chocolate bars and whatnot. Civic service was ultimately required after being caught.

Fortunately, it also included some more legitimate pursuits like outdoor camping at the Little Red River Provincial Park four kilometres north of the city. One such adventure found us camped on one of its several islands. I was 11 years old and my brother and his friend Walter Pronto were 13. We had our 22 rifles and a 20-lb bow. We slept under the stars, waking just long enough to stoke the fire. The next morning they left me with the weapons and went off to their own adventures, returning a day later. And while this seems unusual in our current age of pedophiles and crime scene investigations, it wasn't that unusual for us. At 11 you were pretty much old enough to fend for your self in the bush and use a small rifle, albeit in the near range of home. In fact, there were times we were sent in the summer to live and work on the farms of friends and relatives. During these periods we would make a point of playing in the bush and blazing trails to find one another. On one such occasion we lost Mark. But we found him the next day using a team of horses to extend our search. Use of dogs, rifles and small tractors pulling the requisite water barrels to destroy gophers was an endless summer pursuit on the farms when chores weren't required.

Living on the edge of hooliganism as we were in those years in "P.A." was a necessary distraction from home. Home. Our comparatively modern house on 21st Street was increasingly the scene of intense domestic violence. What was started in Canwood was being perfected in Prince Albert. One particularly memorable Christmas the tirade and beating ended with the Christmas tree being ripped up from its precarious stand and thrown out the door, Christmas ornaments and all. It rested unceremoniously cocked to one side on the snowdrift by the front step. The presents remained, thankfully. Needless to say, the joy of opening them was greatly diminished the next morning, as they were opened with one eye on the gift and one on the body language of our captor, who demanded a sense of normalcy for the opening process. It's amazing the sense of normalcy that can be maintained in the face of insanity when required.

Mom taught at the John Diefenbaker School, newly built in the new area of town. By all accounts she was a great teacher and very well liked. My Dad taught in the Catholic school system. By all accounts there was a good deal of conflict at his work place, primarily imposed by him, I would think. Dad didn't get stress, he gave it. The accolades my mother got for her teaching prowess, coupled with his own struggles, may have served as a source of contention that created the one-sided domestic violence that ensued in P.A. (not that it took much). Who knows?

My older brother Doug was increasingly away from home because of the violence. The reason for being away was probably also related to the fact that he witnessed a late afternoon beating of my mom over a trivial issue. After Dad had left the scene he explained to mom that if he ever saw this again he was going to kill Dad. Unfortunately Dad was just outside on the step "cooling off." He heard every word and returned in to the kitchen, his face flushed, ready to fight his 13-year-old son. Doug was pushed and slammed around. A few bruises but nothing big came out of it—no broken bones or anything. Doug slept outside in the Ford Falcon after that.

It wasn't that Doug wasn't capable of killing somebody. I mean, he wasn't the kind of guy you would want to make angry. Maybe that's what he had in mind when he took a shot at me in Medstead with a 30:30 rifle. I was two and Doug came in to our small kitchen with Dad's hunting rifle. He aimed in our direction (Mom was feeding me in the high chair) and pulled the trigger, not knowing that the rifle had been loaded by Mark the day before. It was like a blast of dynamite went off in the room. The bullet flew right through my mom's leg and into the wall beside her. In the stunned silence after the blast Mom's leg erupted in blood. My Dad applied a tourniquet quickly and Mom was rushed off to the hospital. While Mom was the victim, I'm not sure if I wasn't the target. So, needless to say, I had a healthy respect for Doug's anger mode, a mode that was to continue for most of his early adult life.

The home violence became a constant source of anxiety for all of us, my father excluded, of course. I remember sitting in my Grade 5 classrooms on the second floor of King

George V elementary, poised and anxiously attentive to the slam of cars doors and muffled voices of individuals at ground floor level below. Their voices were rising and falling as the situation demanded communication. I listened anxiously, fearing it was another "knock-down drag-out fight" between Mom and Dad, and, as in times past, I was to be dragged home from class to "make a choice of who I was siding with." Are you staying with Mom or Dad? Decision time, boy—who's it going to be? (It was generally understood that a choice for the wrong team would be fatal.) Of course, all the kids made the right choice. We were young, not stupid. And mother would admit to being the source of all evil. My gut wrenched with fear every time I heard even faint sounds below my fifth-grade window that might be early signs of this type of event. Each time the voices faded without incident, but the fear remained. So I watched and listened, gazing out the window for long periods at a stretch. Unfortunately, my teacher thought I was nuts.

Whatever the reason, the at-home violence was hard, fast and continuous. Our stormy relationship with the PAOC continued in P.A. My father found no satisfaction with the PAOC and, filled with equal discontent over his teaching career and feeling the need to develop "his ministry," made some considerable decisions. It was decided that we were to live on faith while he launched his "Power Unlimited" ministry. It worked for Oral Roberts and would work for us too. Teaching to make money was just a carnal distraction that was preventing him from doing what God had called him to do.

So, with little fanfare, Power Unlimited was launched and the entire family began living on faith on 21st Avenue. An old brick warehouse type building was selected in downtown P.A. for the fledgling church and chairs and a podium were purchased. We even had a piano, somehow. And, of course, the entire family—now consisting of two parents and six kids—attended, and attended, and attended. Unfortunately, that was all who attended. And while the charade played out over several months, the attending faithful said nothing. Fortunately there was no mention of Kool-Aid—if there were, we would have drunk it.

The bills continued to mount on the home front, supplemented of course by the cost of the new church rental. Month after month this continued, until finally even Dad had to face the facts. Not that any of us would consider helping him come to the conclusion that our step of faith was a failure. Just attend church keep your mouth shut and go to school, or anywhere other than home, for that matter, whenever you could.

Then once again God "called" us to move.

Before doing so, a replacement vehicle was needed for our ailing Ford Falcon. It had seen many a hard mile endured at the hands of our modern-day Jehu at the wheel. New beginnings demanded a new vehicle. How we got it no one knows, except to say that perhaps American Motors was just a little too anxious to enter the North American car market. Whether an authentic miracle to spur us on our way or the product of over-eager investment gurus, the fact is we got a brand new 660 Rambler Classic station wagon—white exterior with red interior, and even a padded dash (a padded dash could be helpful). It had red carpets with leg level accent lights, adjustable front seats, soft and padded red vinyl seats with black pinstripes, a fold-down back seat, and under the hood was a smooth-purring 263 cubic inch V8. It rode like a dream, at least in comparison to the old Falcon. Hey, when you spend a lot of time in your parent's car you remember it. And that we did.

Doug ran away from home just after we got it. It was during the Rambler's first big test flight to a Bible camp near Meadow Lake, SK. He had disappeared for several days, hitchhiking south. His departure added to the normal tension. Spurred on by the desire to keep Doug at home, my father decided to return to PA and try to find Doug. Doug was eventually located in a nearby town and returned home.

We moved two months later to Hinton, Alberta.

9: Hinton

MAYBE IT WAS THE BOOMTOWN ATMOSPHERE of Alberta and the Hinton area; maybe it was the fact that everyone in town was new to this thriving pulp mill community; maybe it was the new setting in the looming presence of the Rocky Mountains. Whatever the reason, Hinton was certainly a short but welcome change, a time of rest and renewal for a battered and besieged family—brief but refreshing. Dad taught at the local high school.

Most likely, for members of the family, it was all the factors mentioned above. For my father, however, it was most likely the fact that he had now connected with a charismatic non-denominational church group in Edmonton. This group offered a new spiritual start separate and apart from the PAOC organization that had by now branded him as a troublemaker—a reputation he had come to deserve.

For a time the contact and fellowship he enjoyed with this new group brought spiritual renewal and satisfaction to his life. It also brought it to us as kids, as I recall. I, for one, soaked up the new exposure to people who seemed genuinely full of faith and compassion. The presence of God in the meetings we attended seemed palpable. You felt it, at least I did.

Sundays always meant a long trip in to Edmonton from Hinton, six kids and two adults packed into the station wagon for a five-hour trip. Meetings all day Sunday, then dinner at a local restaurant before our long journey back home. Most often we would arrive home very late Sunday night. The town just before Hinton when returning from Edmonton was appropriately named Obed—oh, we were ready for bed when we got home! By the time we got there, my younger brother Brock would be fast asleep, or so he would lead us to believe. My thought was he faked it so he would be carried in to bed by Dad each time. Kids are kind of shallow.

With our father happy with a new-found spiritual fulfillment, we thoroughly integrated with new friends and classmates. We explored the many local parks and enjoyed unlimited access to hockey, Jasper Park, Miette Hot Springs and the local creeks and waterfalls. It was a 12-year-old's dream. My best friend, Guy Godine, lived across the street. Two doors down lived Ricky Armstrong, friend number two. We spent many hours over at Ricky's place watching the classics like "F Troop" and "Bonanza" on the first colour TV in the neighbourhood. Saturday morning was for watching cartoons at Guy's. Our ancient TV didn't work by that time, so watching at our house wasn't an option, though should it have been technically possible in the new atmosphere at home, then this would have been fine.

Hinton was pretty much a record in my mind. It involved one and a half years of non-violence in the home. Peace, you might say. It was also where we were exposed to other genuine Christians in a non-confrontational setting, where Christian faith translated into healing and acceptance for our father and us. Being accepted by a body of believers for the first time was a paradigm shift for us that remains strongly in our memory.

Unfortunately, it was just the calm before the big storm.

Storms on the prairies are preceded by a gathering blackness. The warm sun of the day is pushed aside by towering blue-black storm clouds, building ever higher on the horizon until by late afternoon they fill the sky. In their path the wind, suddenly chilled, whips up the dust of the prairie roads. The distant rumble of thunder ominously announces the coming storm. With wild abandon, the storm unleashes all its fury, testing all fixtures, features and fools crazy enough to be caught exposed.

It started with the discovery of persons who were less than perfect at the church in Edmonton, which led to a violent confrontation with several of the church elders in the foyer. The loud shouting and slamming that ensued migrated down to the Sunday School in the basement where we waited with bated breath. On Dad's arrival we were loudly ordered out of the building to the station wagon waiting for us in the parking lot. We left town in a hurry, never to return to that church again. This led to renewed isolation, and inevitably to Dad trying to exercise his ministry by preaching to the kids in his high school class—in fact, not allowing them to leave until he was done speaking well after the class had ended. Doug was again one of those students and, finding the ensuing ridicule and shame more than he cold bear, he struck out on his own. He left home first in 1965. He made it to Claresholm, AB, where he stayed with friends. Eventually he was found by us and he returned. Again exposed to the school circus situation, and feeling it was more than he could take, he left for good in May, 1966, at age 16. Unknown to us, he headed for Vancouver and connected with friends he knew from P.A. and our Aunt Kay. Aunt Kay took him in at first. He worked in Richmond at Andy's gardening service and when he had enough to get by he lived on his own there. He connected with local bikers and assorted friends. True to heritage he worked hard but he also partied hard. In a few short years, his arrest record grew to be "the length of your arm," as they say.

——10: Transients

THE FALLOUT AT THE SCHOOL meant we were on the road again. Usually this meant a search for "greener pastures," a.k.a. a teaching assignment somewhere else. Not this time. This time it meant living on faith again, only this time with no particular place to preach. It meant living in hotels in Edmonton with Dad trying to connect to Christian ministries in town. The first hotel was the Chateau Lacombe with full room service. Not bad digs for poor people. Dad had taken up the habit of writing cheques on faith by now. The cheque to the Chateau Lacombe bounced as high as the penthouse, and it's a tall hotel. We were out of there after three weeks. It was then on to the Edmonton Inn and another three weeks in there before they figured out they weren't getting paid. Apparently God hadn't been informed that it was his job to cover that cheque either. We ended up at the Pan American Hotel just down Kingsway from the Edmonton Inn in the lower-rent district. We got one of those self-contained units I think they built in the '40s before the motel upgraded to a Hotel—two bedrooms, a kitchenette and a small living room. Mom was expecting her seventh child, Chris, so she was very much incapacitated. We weren't fortunate enough to get room service. The restaurant went on a strictly cash and carry basis. The end result of that and new prolonged absences from Dad meant there were many days we went hungry, with no food for several days at a stretch and no sign of Dad. Rhonda and I prayed for food for the kids and God answered. One of the ladies at the restaurant felt compelled to take some food over to our unit out of the blue. To you that might not be God—just circumstance—but to us it was a miracle, plain and simple.

Dad returned to the now-desperate circumstance. The press of hungry kids, another on the way, and the fact that God had still not opened up some ministry opportunity obviously made him extremely angry. Naturally he took it out first on Mom and then us. She was beaten black and blue, a broom handle broken over her back as she crawled across the floor, then kicked repeatedly. Still the anger was not vented so he started on us.

Chris was born soon after at the Royal Alexandria Hospital in 1967. We (the kids) named him Christopher Elliot after Elliot Ness of "The Untouchables." I guess Dad had run out of names by then.

The seriousness of the situation was obvious, even to Dad. We were going to get kicked out of the Pan American pretty soon and faith had failed to provide. Decision time: would we go back to teaching, welfare or what?

Dad went out to Stony Plain in response to an ad for a teacher at Seba Beach, not far down the road from Edmonton. On a late August afternoon all of us sat in the buzzing heat in the car outside the District Office waiting for Dad to return. Its times like these you become reacquainted with every knob, dial and button in the car. Seemed like years but it was only hours. Nevertheless, Dad returned and confirmed they had offered him a position. The look on his face was strained, with a hint of insanity I remember to this day. Would he decide to take it and the money this offered, or stick to his living-on-faith plan? He turned to Mom and asked her to decide.

The Bible has a verse in Revelation that says there was silence in Heaven for half an hour before judgement was to be pronounced. This was one of those times. With six hungry kids in the car and a 16-year-old as a runaway, Mom said haltingly she thought we should take it. A cold silence descended.

We moved our limited belongings to Seba Beach shortly after. Dad bought living room furniture on credit. We only touched down in Seba Beach for a stormy six months. Dad was again torn between this carnal work and "his ministry" calling. To add to that, he frequently pointed to the fact that it was "all your mother's idea to move here. I wanted to go on faith, but no, your mother wanted this."

Seba Beach was a resort town and the population was correspondingly transient, much like us. We never made friends there, and the people never missed us when we left.

We touched down in Calgary, living briefly in a furnished three-bedroom rancher in central Calgary. Our furniture stayed behind for now until Dad could find a job. It caught up with us briefly when we rented a half-duplex in southwest Calgary. Unfortunately, it was all repossessed shortly thereafter. With the furniture gone, it made the place look big—empty, but big. The Rambler was taken for a lien for some repairs we had done a short time earlier. Dad was working in sales and was away from home for extended periods. He had an old '56 Ford Fairlane for his traveling and would be gone for weeks at a stretch.

Money was in short supply, so I took up a job selling things door to door. It gave me some money. Unfortunately, or perhaps fortunately, I didn't get to spend it. Dad would come home and take it all. He'd first ask for it, but if I hesitated he'd say he was taking it anyway. I'm not sure what it was spent on, but it wasn't a whole lot anyway. I'm not sure why I kept earning it either. Maybe having it for short periods of time was a reward in itself. We never spent money on ourselves—it just wasn't done. Besides, if it went to the family, that was good enough.

Not having Dad around much was pretty much a plus. No violence, just school and some work after school, and one good friend. It was almost peaceful. Still, we had little to eat and less to sit on. This lasted to the end of the Grade 7 school year, and when the landlord insisted on rent we moved to Sylvan Lake. The '56 Ford died about then and we upgraded to a '54 Buick. We lived in a big old house a few blocks from the Sylvan Lake beach. It was 1967. I remember that because it was the time of the 1967 war in Israel. My Dad was at least right about that one. It looked pretty bleak for Israel at the start but Dad predicted they would have to win to fulfill Biblical prophecy and all. And he was right. They snatched victory from the jaws of defeat. Needless to say we were well schooled in Biblical prophecy. And even if we didn't pay our bills and wrote fraudulent cheques, we at least had the course of history figured out.

Anyways, my dad continued to try and make a go of it with sales. He did work at it. I helped a biny o driving for him. Sometimes he'd say, "You drive and I'll just rest my eyes a bit." He'd be so tired from pounding the pavement all day that he'd fall right to sleep. I'd just drive. I was 13 but I knew how to drive from working on the farms in summer. I'd just drive till we got home.

Never got caught either.

11: Vilna and the Resurrection of the 660

MANY OF THE FEROCIOUS STORMS that emerge on the prairies are preceded by a calm that lulls the eventual participants in the storm events to complacency, a complacency that works to the favour of the destructive nature of the coming event. So it was in Vilna, our next stop.

The community of Vilna was two hours northeast of Edmonton, a rural community founded by Ukrainian Canadians who settled in the area in the early 1900s. A main street (mandatory for prairie towns) dominated the town with small shops and stores of every description lined along its sides, each shop and store the product of the individual entrepreneurial spirit of the local Ukrainian Canadian population. No big-box multinational conglomerates here, just one main hotel and several gas stations. It was a three-elevator town, which meant a higher status than some of the smaller surrounding towns. It boasted a hospital, a theatre, a seed cleaning plant and a train station where actual passengers were loaded and unloaded on the VIA rail service. They never used the "all aboard" vernacular, but you got the same feeling of awe from the event nevertheless.

The homes in town were usually small, many of them very small and very old, but all immaculately kept with gardens to die for. Many of the seniors were resident in these small homes since retiring from their farms and held the care with which they were maintained in high regard. They made poppy seed cakes and assorted cookies and pies that would be the envy of Martha Stewart. Kielbasa was made locally and sold in the local cafés. The new generation farmed the land intensely and earnestly. Hardworking, honest and generous these people were. They had carved this civilized existence out of a hard and sometimes bitterly cold landscape. Without knowing it, they were the epitome of the hard-working immigrant force that shaped Canada.

For us, things got better. We lived in a small house about six miles out of town; what it lacked in size, it made up for in outdoor amenities. It came complete with our very own farm. Not that we were running the farm, but we could certainly play on it to our hearts' content. There was the smallish red barn with white trim that sat empty but beckoned us to explore it. We slid back the heavy wooden doors, and once our eyes adjusted to the internal gloom, we could see the wooden stalls where cattle had been housed standing at attention in neat rows. The heavy wooden posts and walls, worn smooth in places from years of wear, stuck out of the concrete foundation, cool even on a mid-day summer's heat. A worn wooden ladder led us up to the hayloft, where the bright sun shone through the large windows at the end of the loft. Dust, left from years of hay storage and disturbed by our presence, rose and danced lazily in the sunlight's broad golden shaft.

A row of granaries lined the north end of the farmyard. Two tractors were situated 50 yards from the back porch; a seed drill, harrows and a plow set rounded out the machinery list. There was lots to play on.

The house was another matter. A small, matter-of-fact kitchen, complete with a pump handle in the sink—no running water. A large coal heater in the center of the tiny living room served to warm the house, if you fed it often. Small bedrooms where we slept in close quarters, eight of us in two bedrooms. The small washroom held a toilet, complete with waste bucket underneath, and washing basin. It was pretty basic. Still, in our minds the external amenities more than compensated for what the house failed to offer. I'm sure our parents didn't agree.

Nevertheless, we had landed safely after our sojourn in Calgary/Sylvan Lake. We had a roof over our heads with a feeling of permanence. Both Mom and Dad were teaching in town, making up for financial lost ground. As a result we soon got new furniture. Nothing fancy—a naugahyde couch and chair—but it beat sitting on the floor. The couch made into a double bed for two to sleep in the living room. A new bunk bed made sleeping four boys to a room easier.

To round out the turn of events Dad eventually got the Rambler 660 out of hock for the repairs that had been done. It arrived one afternoon and we all piled in for old time's sake. It was like the return of a long lost pet. Its arrival afforded us a renewed sense of confidence that all would be well again.

This respite allowed us to recover financially and emotionally from 18 months of hard going. We used the oldest of the two tractors to tour the farm and explore the fields and nearby roads. I managed to get the old Buick stuck in one of those fields and Dad used the tractor to pull it out. He didn't even get mad. Rhonda learned to drive in the old Buick on the back roads despite our back seat coaching. One memorable event had her having to choose between turning left and turning right at a Y in the road. With all of us shouting different directions out of the back seat, she managed to do neither, depositing the big hulk of a car in the ditch between the two alternatives. We piled out of the back seat, leaving her crying behind the wheel, and set out for home on foot, which we determined to be much safer.

Six miles of walking made us wonder at times if we did the right thing. Dad got a tractor from a local farmer and pulled her out. I recall they passed us on our forced march home with Rhonda smiling at us as she rode by in the comfort of the Buick's deep padded seats. Road dust in our teeth, we trudged on.

But the bliss of our brief stay at the farmhouse was shattered late one fall evening as a pail full of coal went through the living room window, signalling the beginning of a new phase of domestic violence. Who knows what alignment of planets would trigger these things? For us it was a mystery that added to the terror of the experience. It may have been problems on the job for my father, or something of a compliment to my mother for her teaching ability by some well intentioned idiot who of course would have no idea of the string of grief that such an act could precipitate. This lifestyle made one wary of even the slightest disturbance in the Force, and one could irrationally blame all manner of external and ultimately related incidents (we are all connected) for instigating Round 42. But no matter the source, once initiated, the fighting was all that mattered. This one went on for days and culminated in us driving down the highway towards town at high forward speed and my father ramming the column shift on the automatic transmission into reverse. The Rambler literally arched in full flight, the tires contacting the pavement for short periods with associated screeching and burning rubber. Eventually it slowed. My father shifted in to forward and then reverse repeatedly as we slowed to halt. So much for that transmission. Later expertise suggested to me that this could have put equal strain on the crankshaft and differential. But hey, it stopped us dead in our tracks anyway. In times like those you didn't mind Dad stomping off into the distance. Your only hope was that he would not come back. He didn't that day. I recall we waited by the side of the road clutching our lunch bags for school until a pickup truck arrived and drove us into town.

The consequence of all this may not have been readily apparent to us all as we rode in to town that day. Amongst other things, it meant we didn't get along much with our current landlord for the farm due to the damage at home, and the now-permanent demise of the Rambler meant our transportation options were limited, the old Buick being unsuitable for winter driving. These factors conspired to have us move into town.

The place chosen for our new residence was the rather old and run down train station. This old relic was built in the '40's when train was king. It had seen better days. Still, it was solidly built. It had a small, attached room identified as a kitchen with wooden pantries lining the north wall. These were home to a number of mice that had to be kept at bay with traps and a hand pellet gun we eventually acquired. The sink and counter were rudimentary, but there was a water tap and drain, signifying the return of running water and sewer to our lives. These meant that the upstairs bathroom was also plumbed, a welcome relief after the farm. The living room and dining area were one large room. At the west end a staircase led upstairs, where there were three large bedrooms and the aforementioned washroom. Downstairs was the darkest, dankest basement in living memory that housed a coal furnace and coal room. The grates in the furnace had burned out from long-term use. The pipes from this old behemoth led up to the upper floors. Assorted old bottles and tanks littered the downstairs landscape. The rest of the station housed the waiting area for the passenger trains that hurtled by, stopping every second pass or so. This waiting area was accessible by a door now bolted shut. The waiting area was warmed by a modern oil stove heater and was lined each side by officious-looking hard wood benches that served the waiting public. The waiting area led onto a broad wooden platform that paralleled the track for about 60 feet. A station warehouse rounded out the appointments with heavy sliding doors opening to a cavernous old storage area that was also accessible from a platform. While water and sewer were a big domestic advantage, the external amenities were definitely lacking. Wedged between the tracks and the gravel road adjacent to the downtown, there was little room for six kids to play. We had to go further afield for recreational activity.

A definite positive advantage of our new location was the fact that it was a short 5-block walk to school. That made us masters of our own destiny in that department—no more wild rides with Dad at the helm of the vehicle on our way to school. Under our own direction, arrival on time was assured.

We fanned out in every direction in the days after our arrival. Over time we built a new tree fort a half-mile down the tracks with stolen building materials from the adjacent elevators. It was a Radloff boys' project all around. Even Paul, then only five, chipped in, dragging materials twice his weight down the track, foreshadowing the worker he would come to be later in life. For this he was rewarded by being allowed to smoke cigars with us in the completed fort.

We shared one bike between all of us and used it to connect with some friends we had made in town. We used the local rink extensively in the ensuing winter because it was free. We'd play from dawn till dusk most Saturdays and from after school till dark most weeknights. We weren't allowed to play on Sunday, of course.

Sometimes we'd arrive early Saturday morning to play only to find the snow had drifted in overnight, covering the corners and sections of center ice with hardened snow sloping upwards and over the wooden boards. We'd get right to work and shovel it out before we played, even if it took several hours. A lack of a working TV at home was a great motivator for our shovelling efforts.

Sometimes the Radloff kids would form the entire team when the local kids showed up. It was us against them. Rhonda got to play goal. It was an unwritten rule around our place that she, being the only girl of the family, must not come home from our adventures harmed. So we played exceptional defence to assure that this would be the case.

Brock and I would often play long after everyone else had gone home. We'd head for home only when either hunger or numbing cold motivated us to do so. On occasion we'd skate home on the hard compact snow on the roads, our fingers too numb to unlace our skates.

Ah, yes—home. Home was taking on surreal characteristics. Dad was bad now, repeating himself constantly, sometimes repeating a phrase seven or eight times. You'd have to wait for him to do it until he got the exact right feeling from the phrase, not an easy task some days. We had church in the house, too, since we just had the now-very-old Buick, and it wasn't reliable for long trips into Edmonton where the larger charismatic churches were. The service would go on forever, it seemed; some singing followed by hours of Dad preaching at us. You wouldn't dare move. Dad evidently tried convincing some of the kids he taught from school to drop by but they never came. Eventually this badgering of kids about their faith brought "persecution" from the principal. And in the not-too-distant future Dad was suspended. This in turn got us into renewed financial trouble. It also served to crank up the bizarre repetition behaviour and escalated the family violence. He also increased the lecture lengths to unbearable proportions. I remember sitting one night in front of our meagre supper and not being allowed to eat until his lecture was done. We sat for hours unable to move or eat until some of the kids began to cry.

I remember about then I started to sleep with a knife under my pillow. Hearing the shouting and beatings taking place downstairs, I sat in my bed on several occasions gripping the knife handle and preparing to go downstairs to kill my father. I used to read news stories about boys who did such things and follow them to see how much jail time they got. While I planned and plotted, the beatings continued. Eventually Mom was not allowed to teach at the school, as it looked bad to my dad that they accepted her and not him.

Dad was caught for impaired driving just north of Smokey Lake when he and I were driving home in the Buick. I don't remember him stopping for a drink but it could have happened: who knew what he'd do when we were left in the car? I testified for him at the trial (he insisted on representing himself) but he was convicted anyway. Having no money to pay he did time in jail in Edmonton. I remember them taking him away while I wondered how I'd get home to Vilna, having no money myself. I think I hitchhiked back. My hitchhiking experience when I was five came in handy.

After doing some time Dad came home. We had very little in the house. He arrived with a friend he'd met in jail. A young man we were told to call James. He lived with us and shared what little we had. He and Dad would go into to Edmonton on occasion together, leaving us at home—not a bad thing for us, really.

About this time my oldest brother Mark became very ill with pneumonia-type symptoms. Mark had been going downhill for some time mentally and physically due to lack of proper medical care and the cumulative effects of his epileptic seizures. They seemed to be more severe and prolonged now. He was not allowed out of the yard for these reasons. One of us was always assigned to "take care of Mark." Being assigned thus meant no time spent with friends so the task was split up equally between Brock, Rhonda and me. Paul and Chris were too young for this assignment. Once assigned, the task was not too difficult because Mark, though twice our size, was very gentle and unassuming. He was content to chase you in the yard, limping on his disabled left side until you let him catch you. He'd say, "You be the pigs and I'll be the wolf," before each chase. After some time of this he would play out and be more content with breaking twigs he would either find on the ground or take from the willow bushes behind the house. Mark was thoroughly happy when he could spend his time with us like this. His mental capabilities were much diminished from earlier years. Physically he was pale and emaciated.

Given his existing physical condition and tendencies for seizures, when he got pneumonia it was serious, so serious my mother begged my father to let Doctor Frobe look at him and have him admitted to the hospital if necessary. Dad refused on the simple grounds that we needed to have faith and God had showed him that Mark would be healed in his ministry.

What Dad did decide is that he needed to take us kids in to Klondike Days in Edmonton. James didn't want to go like the rest of us but eventually, over protests from my mother and James, we were all loaded into the old Buick and set out for Edmonton. All except Mark, who lay in the double bed in the boys' room next to my single bed, and my mother who remained to tend to Mark. As we pulled out on to the main highway I had a sudden sense that Mark was about to die. This was unusual, as at the time I didn't think it was that serious given our pending trip.

On our arrival home that night I remember Mom meeting Dad in the kitchen. She was sobbing, but between sobs she managed to tell Dad that Mark was dead. He had died shortly after we had left that morning. My father fell to his knees on the floor between the kitchen and the living room and wept himself. I had a strange sense of peace that Mark was okay, and since I had sensed he was dead before, was not shocked by this event. I was saddened by the loss of my brother who I had prayed God to help just days before, but not shocked.

Dad felt differently. After the initial impact of the moment was spent, he rose to his feet. He wavered and paced about the living room and dining room, grieving at one moment, casting blame in the next. Then, with great determination, he announced his revelation that God would raise Mark from the dead immediately—we just needed to pray for him in faith. Now at this I was shocked. My mother sat frozen to her chair in the kitchen, the magnitude of this statement running through her mind. It was like time suspended for a moment while rational thought struggled against the meaning of the words. Eventually rational thought succumbed to the mission before us. We were to raise Mark up from the dead that night.

We found ourselves gathered around Mark in the double bed in our room. The walls were greyed with age and stooped in one corner to conform to the gable roof arrangement of the house. One window sat over my bed. It looked out first over the shakes on the roof that covered the loading platform and ultimately over the tracks that gleamed in the late summer moon. The air was already cool in the clear evening.

Mark's bare and lifeless body, pale and emaciated, lay on the bed. The checkerboard quilt, made by my mother from scraps of material and worn from years of wear, lay over the lower half of his body. We watched my father attempt alternating methods of resurrection, starting with laying on hands and prayer, and that failing, resorting to artificial respiration and applying warm towels to the body. We were forced to assist in all these methods. We were encouraged to confirm how Mark looked better and revived in response to our efforts. Of course, we agreed this was the case. This despite the cold, obviously stiffening body before us. This continued on late into the night. Good thing it was late summer and there was no school tomorrow. Finally, exhausted from these efforts and with the younger ones falling asleep on their knees, we were forced to accept sleep. We were to continue tomorrow.

The younger kids, already asleep, were carried to Rhonda's room across the hall. Mom and Dad and Chris slept in our parent's room down the hall. Brock and I slept in my bed with Mark in the other bed next to us. While this was usually unacceptable under normal circumstances, tonight it was OK. Brock was asleep in minutes. I fell asleep with the POOL elevator across the tracks illuminated by the moon, which had fled to the other side of the house. The slats of the elevator's wooden structure were illuminated on its giant frame, looming and somehow livened by the brilliant moonlight, and yet still and cold like the pale frame next to us.

We awoke the next morning to a renewed effort. This effort was initiated at about 11 a.m. with only me and Brock assisting Dad. My mom watched silently from the edge of my bed. A pain deeper than the death of her son registered on her face. She was deeply tired and drawn. She seemed to be in another world. We wished we were also.

I don't recall all that happened that day. I do recall that after many hours of this exercise Dad admitted temporary defeat. There was only one person running the show now. Mom was too withdrawn to even offer comment. Most of my dad's thoughts were directed to myself, I guess, as I was the oldest present. I didn't argue, but felt strange with the new level to which I was being confided in. The assistant captain of the doomed Titanic might have felt the same way.

A decision to abandon ship was made. To Dad, this meant we would all pile in the car and with whatever belongings we had we would go to Edmonton tomorrow where he could think this through. That night we slept again as the night before, but with a difference.

My mother, despondent over the death of her son, had prayed herself to sleep. She had one prayer: that was that God would show her that her son was safe. Not an easy assumption, given the collective wisdom of most of the churches that Mark's seizures were a sign of demonic possession. She later remembered praying this specifically before she went to sleep. She felt an assurance that this would be done for her.

Early the next morning, she awoke to a very vivid dream. In that dream she dreamt Mark was walking back and forth on wispy clouds before Jesus. He was walking normally now and smiling. Jesus was smiling, too, and was saying to Mark, "You can really do it now, can't you, Mark?" Mark was very happy and walked all the more in response to this encouragement. She awoke with a start. On remembering the dream she paused to thank the Lord for this confirmation. It was what she needed to get through the day.

Just then Rhonda came quickly into the room. She had awakened at the same time and she excitedly told Mom about a vivid dream she had just had. She could hardly contain her excitement, so Mom asked her to relate the source of this excitement. She hurriedly related that in her dream she saw Mark walking on wispy clouds before Jesus. Jesus was sitting on a rock and Mark was walking in front of him normally. No more limp. Jesus was telling Mark, "You can really do it now, can't you, Mark?" to which Mark responded by walking more vigorously. Mom wept, but was strengthened immediately. Rhonda cried with her. It was a bond that was to hold them close together for many years.

We left for Edmonton. Mark lay in the bed, left behind for the last time. Eventually the authorities came to remove the body. I am told the smell from the body was overpowering. His body decomposed to the point that a closed casket was required at the subsequent funeral.

The funeral was not well attended, just a few friends of the family. There were no flowers. We sat in the front row with a pastor officiating. I sat looking down to my feet, glancing up occasionally at the dark wood casket. My father sat upright and was attentive to the proceedings. He began to become agitated towards the closing of the proceedings. Without warning, he shot across the short strip of carpet between the casket and us and attempted to open the casket. Restrained by the pastor and the funeral home manager, he called to Mark, "Markey, get up!" He explained that Mark was to rise from the dead and repeated his calls to Mark. Eventually he was assisted to be seated, only to go through the same procedure again. We sat embarrassed for Mark and ourselves. Eventually the casket was wheeled out and Mark was placed in the hearse. We followed behind in a large black Cadillac to the graveyard in Northeast Edmonton. There, with the sound of vehicles rushing by, the casket was laid in to the cold moist earth.

After the funeral Dad became more unstable and irrational, repeating his sentences and driving to and from destinations. He returned from one of his frequent departures late one afternoon to a home where we were staying in Edmonton. Within moments he was arguing with Mom and flew in to a rage. He seized a butcher knife from the drawer in the kitchen and lunged towards her. From nowhere, the lady of the house, who happened to be a psychiatric nurse, appeared and, taking the top of his sport coat with both hands, pulled the coat down, immobilizing his arms. The knife dropped from his hands, bouncing on the linoleum floor. Her husband came to her aid. Dad fled the scene. The police were called and eventually he was ordered to have a psychiatric assessment. When complete, the psychiatrist declared him to be "as sane as I am." In retrospect this makes one seriously wonder about this psychiatrist specifically and the science of psychiatry generally. But Dad did some time. While he was away we returned home to Vilna.

On our return we attempted to get back to normal. This was to be short lived, however, as Dad soon returned home with another young native man called Frank. They arrived in a rented Chevy Chevelle. Nice car, though I wasn't sure how we could afford to rent it with us having little or no money and all. Actually, we were on welfare at that point, so renting automobiles was not feasible. It wasn't clear however who was paying for this car. What was to become clear was that Dad and this man were having a relationship, which played out most nights after the younger kids were asleep. They stayed together in my sister's room for several nights. Rhonda stayed in Mom's room. After several days of this Frank left.

It was a Friday night at the end of August, and hot for that time of year. I had left home to hang out with my friends down at Andy's café. It was a good hangout for us. You could get cigarettes for five cents a piece, which was great because you couldn't afford a whole pack. There was a jukebox and arcade games that ate any change we had left after cigarettes. The booths would seat four. The brown vinyl seats were worn and cracked with the stuffing showing in places. I got called outside about 9 p.m. by one of the town kids who told me I needed to go home right away. Of course, I said I would go later, when we were done at the café. He told me things were bad at home and I should go home right away. I stumbled off down the dark alley that parallels the main street. Walking any great speed was a challenge. The only sound was the sound of the gravel kicked up by my shoes in the darkness. On arriving at the end of the alley my eyes adjusted to the light of the mercury vapour streetlight that whined in the silence above me. Peering over at the house for the next leg of my journey I could see that something was definitely wrong. There in the dim shadows that engulfed the station courtyard sat four shiny new police cruisers. They were empty but idling quietly. Their silence was interrupted briefly by the squeaky chatter of the radios. I pushed past them to the house entrance. I could make out several officers standing in the kitchen. The shadows of several more in the living room brushed up against the windows as they moved about.

There in the doorway between the kitchen and the living room sat my father. He sat with a tea towel draped over a hammer that was propping him up off the ground. His back was to the doorframe. He was conversing with the sergeant who towered over him. The house was pretty much totalled. Everything from cups to saucers to lay in pieces on the floor. The cupboards were all smashed in tiny pieces, the chairs the same. The piano laid in rubble, its piano wires evident through the splintered maple casing. A few of the felt covered piano hammers stood raised as if frozen in place, their attempts to strike a more peaceful chord suspended forever. Some of their less fortunate mates were strewn across the floor mixed with the debris of tables, chairs, pictures and unrecognizable material. A younger officer, pale and fidgeting, looked nervously over at the sergeant. He had returned from upstairs with news that no one was up there. "Nothing there," he said in relief. His long flashlight was still on despite the glare of the downstairs lights, all on and seemingly glaring either from my adjustment to the higher light level or perhaps bold in the view of carnage they were exposing.

I was ushered out of the house and was seated by myself in the patrol car farthest from the house. The green dash lights and red lights on the radio focused my attention. Spellbound, I stared at them in silence. I feared the worse. My family must be dead. Just like Mark. First Mark, and now them. Worst of all, if they were it was my fault because I wasn't there to protect them when they needed me.

Eventually I was told that they were not dead. The officer explained as he drove me over to Peter David's house where they were staying. Peter David was the "town cop" and involved in the event on an official basis. He lived in a relatively modern house two blocks down from us. There I met Brock and Rhonda. Mom was “resting” in the bedroom and the other kids were sleeping downstairs. My fears were ended. For now.

There I learned what had happened. Dad had waited until I went out after supper. Then with sudden fury he struck. Using the hammer, he began smashing everything in sight. Mom and the kids fled upstairs to Rhonda’s room where they remained. They prayed as the rampage continued downstairs. Over several hours Dad did his work. He systematically destroyed everything with the hammer, yelling and screaming as and when he wanted. He took brief breaks between onslaughts and sat at the table, hammer in hand. During these breaks Brock had ventured partway down the steps from the upstairs and peered into the living room area through the gaps in the railing to see Dad conducting his work. Dad was seething and wild-eyed (some would say crazy). He twitched and spun the hammer in his grip. Brock would return to report the damage and to encourage Mom to leave the house. Mom, like always, refused to leave. It wasn’t done that way in her world. In her world a wife never leaves her husband until death. Brock attempted to relay that death was possibly imminent. My mother stayed and prayed. The rampage ebbed and flowed below.

Brock snuck back to the top edge of the stairs for a final look. On seeing Brock there on the stairs my father hurled the hammer with all his might towards him. It struck the TV near the stairs in flight, shattering the glass. Brock quickly retreated up the stairs to Rhonda’s room. He saw there my mother prying open the sliding window casement, sealed shut from years of disuse. Once freed it slid up, releasing first Brock, then Rhonda, then Mom with Chris in her arms, to the pitched roof over the kitchen add-on. Paul followed up last. Brock and Rhonda were first to manoeuvre to the edge of the roof and down a pole to the ground.

Mom lowered Chris down over the edge of the roof and released him into Brock and Rhonda's arms below. She followed next steadied as she descended down the pole by Brock and Rhonda below. Finally Paul followed down the pole. Safely on the ground they moved quickly through the darkness to Peter David's house. The RCMP was quick to respond. They had arrived shortly before me. Dad told us calmly later he had planned to kill us all that night. The voices he was hearing told him to. He arrived upstairs too late for this to be accomplished.

We were moved to Smokey Lake, not far from Vilna, by the RCMP for our protection. We were housed in a small two-room house near downtown. There we existed in temporary peace. Mom rested most of the time. She was down to 95 pounds, frail and extremely pale. She was taking sedatives. Rhonda and I were in charge of the kids more or less. She did most of the work and I did most of the thinking, mostly about what to do next. There was a real possibility they would break up the family and put us in foster homes, we were told. The RCMP encouraged us to contact our relatives for help. Those who knew our whereabouts were either unable or unwilling to help. Mostly they just didn't know where we were, as Dad had isolated them from us years ago. We had nowhere to turn. Dad was in jail for the present, hopefully with the psychiatrist. But the RCMP advised they couldn't hold him there for much longer. It was Thursday the week before when we got the word he would be coming out of jail on Monday. Something had to be done.

It was the Friday before Dad was to get out of jail. I had gone over the scenario of how to kill my dad with a knife many times in my head. I figured this would have to be done on Monday. I'd wait till he wasn't expecting it and get in as many shots as I could before he turned on me. Or so I thought. Trouble was, every time I went trough this scenario in my head the actual method after the first stab was blurry. This worried me.

That evening Brock and I went out for a walk. There was a light sprinkle of rain. I flicked my cigarette out into the street as we opened the low gate and re-entered the yard. We went into the house and met Rhonda at the kitchen table. The impending arrival of our father was on her mind too.

"Let's pray that someone comes to get us out of here before Dad comes to get us" she said urgently.

I laughed out loud. "Right," I said. "You mean God's going to help us? Look around you. Where's God been?" I snapped. She started to cry. I knew we needed to keep Rhonda on side. She did all the work. So in an effort to keep her happy I said, "Ok, ok, sure, let's pray. I'm sure God will help us out."

She prayed a simple prayer: just, "God, please send someone to take us away from here before Dad gets out of jail. You know what he'll do to us if he gets here so please send someone right away. Amen."

"Great. I'm sure God will send someone to help us," I said. "You feel better now?" I asked, hoping my shallow-sounding response did not impinge on her faith.

She said, "Yes," through a few sniffles. We never spoke about it again. It was Friday night.

Unknown to us, God was at work answering Rhonda's simple prayer. To do so he was using an unlikely character—our brother Doug, who had left home five years earlier. Not that Doug was not up to any challenge. It was just that he had been out of contact with us for a long time. In this five-year period he had developed his own life 1600 kilometres away in Vancouver.

He had arrived there in 1966, staying temporarily with our Aunt Kay. Shortly thereafter he started working for Andy's gardening service based out of Richmond. Like most Radloffs he was a hard worker and he quickly caught on full time. Work was hard and seasonal but he made it on his own. He hung out with a rough crowd of mostly bikers and during that period "Tatter," as he was known by his friends, managed to acquire a long criminal record for drug and assault-related offences. They summarized his record with a bold "V" for violent. I guess in God's mind he had potential.

He was hanging out at Walter Klimash's place near the corner of 37th and Ontario St as usual that Friday night. He was pretty high, having done some cocaine, and was busy following that up with repeat beers. He sat on the bed in Walters's basement apartment listening to their steady dose of Abbey Road, Walter's favourite album. While Doug was sitting there, God spoke to him, clear and plain as day. God said, "Get up."

At first he turned to see who had spoken to him, only slightly awakened from his haze. Then it came again: "Get up now." The voice was strong and demanding. He knew enough to know at that moment who was talking to him. He was completely sober in that moment as he rose to his feet. The voice came again: "Get outside." Maybe God didn't like Abbey Road either.

With that, he started for the door. Walter exclaimed, "Where you going, we're just getting started?"

"Home," Doug said, before he could actually think it through fully. Incredulous, Walter pressed further. "You mean you're going back to Richmond?" Doug lived there in a boarding house.

"No," Doug said. "I'm going home." By that he meant he was going back to Alberta and Walter must have known it. Walter protested, "Home, are you crazy?"

With that, Doug went outside. He didn't go back to Richmond to get anything. Feeling extreme urgency he got into his '62 Mercury convertible and started to drive. Out on the 401 he made serious progress. He drove on all night, arriving in Vilna late Saturday afternoon. With no one at our house he asked around, and after some cross-examination by the RCMP he was told where we were.

Doug arrived at Smokey Lake just after supper. I was sitting on the lawn and watched him roll up. I didn't recognize the car, but when he got out I recognized him. I was stunned. I remember saying, "Sorry, God, for not believing you could do something like that." It was humbling and great all at the same time. From it I learned that no circumstance is beyond His control.

It didn't take long for Doug to get us organized. We put Mom on the train with Brock, Rhonda, Paul and Chris. Doug and I got in the car and headed for Vancouver to meet Mom and the kids there. We went through Calgary and headed through the Rogers Pass to BC.

Mom and the kids arrived before us. Mom and company exited the train station and hailed a cab. "Take us to the cheapest hotel you know of," she directed. They were delivered to the Ambassador Hotel in downtown Vancouver. We met up with Mom and the rest of the kids a day later, and stayed that next night in the hotel in a single room. Doug stayed out at Richmond.

Trying to rent a house in Vancouver in 1969 wasn't easy, particularly for a family of six on welfare, which we were. So after numerous frustrating phone calls to prospective landlords we turned to prayer. We got together just before lunch in the crowded hotel room and prayed that God would open up an opportunity for us to rent a house in a good neighbourhood. Mom led off, with support from Rhonda. Ever the doubting Thomas, I didn't add anything. Doug, as usual for those days, didn't feel qualified to add anything to the request. A short time later we made successful contact with Mr. Fred Drissler, who wished to rent the top floor of his three-bedroom house on 64th and Ash Street in Vancouver. Within minutes we were on our way to see this rental house, all seven of us piled into Doug's Mercury convertible. We were quite a sight, I suppose,

Doug with long hair and leather jacket, Mom all of 90 pounds and looking gaunt and pale, her hair gone completely white, and of course, the rest of us kids with clothes worn and torn. We arrived just as the real estate agent was concluding the deal with Fred to take possession of the house. He glanced out the window at the arrival of the motley crew. Unknown to us the words we could see him mumbling to Fred were: "I know what you might be thinking, but don't be renting this place out to this family." Fred confided later that he had agreed that it would be a bad idea. He left the dining room where he had been signing the last vestiges of paperwork and headed off down to the basement suite he was occupying. He had no intention of letting us rent the place on his way down. On his return from the basement moments later he had completely reversed himself. He told my mother and Doug waiting expectantly in the kitchen that yes, they could rent the house. The Real Estate agent choked and guffawed. Rising with the papers he needed he left with a parting shot that questioned Fred's sanity: "Man, you're nuts." "Welcome to the neighbourhood," he said as he passed Mom and Doug and headed for the door. I wasn't to find out until four years later why Fred changed his mind that day.

Fred was from the old country, Yugoslavia by way of Germany. He and his family were of German descent and were hustled out of Yugoslavia in the care of the German army retreating before the Russians at the close of World War II. His last recollection looking out the back of the lorry taking them out was a long line of Jewish residents strung out along the road in a driving rain. He remembered distinctly the rapid machine gun fire as German soldiers mowed the Jewish citizens down before his eyes. Most of them fell neatly into the ditch beside the road. The Lorry sped on into the driving rain. It stuck in his young memory. Fred's family was relocated to a small village adjacent a death camp in Germany. There he endured steady bomb attacks from the Allied forces and the unmistakeable odour of cooking human remains from the death camp. In his words, there was no way that the local population did not know what was occurring in that camp. All this is to say that Fred may have had good reason to accept a car full of refugees outside. That would be the human answer.

But it wasn't the whole story. The real story was that Fred had gone downstairs that day and encountered the real God that takes care of widows and orphans. Fred told me later that he had just dashed down to get a copy of a document. He had already concluded that, given that he had saved up all his resources to make the house purchase, the real estate agent was right. He would just let them down easy. He recounted that instantly after that thought a great darkness and sense of fear and physical cold came over him, and though he knew nothing of God or any such supernatural existence, he knew that at that point beyond a doubt if he said no to the family waiting above it was not going to go well for him. Fred didn't know the source of this feeling; all he knew was that the consequences of saying no would be death to him. The reason I know about this is that he sought some explanation of this a few years later. Fred would eventually accept this God into his heart the same way I had when I was six.

The net effect of all of this was we had a very nice house to live in and it was in a reasonably nice area of Vancouver. Fred would go on to become like a father to all of us, save Doug, who lived on his own in Richmond. Fred would spend countless hours and all his meagre resources helping the family generally and the boys specifically, taking us skiing, co-signing loans for vehicles, taking us to the World Fair in Spokane and basically doing anything a real father would do for his kids.

——12: The Empire Strikes Back

LIKE DARTH VADER, leader of the evil empire, Dad emerged from prison seething at the escape of the forces of rebellion. He set on a quest to find us. Unlike Darth, who had to search the universe, my father's search could reasonably be confined to western Canada. This he did with the aid of his "Secretary," a woman who provided all the resources he needed to conduct the search. It took approximately a year and a half for him to find us late one evening parked across the street from the house. Needless to say this instilled a chill of fear on us all. He probed our defences cautiously at first, sitting across the street from the house and later calling the house. His demands quickly escalated, insisting on seeing Paul and Chris, threatening if that was not arranged he would take them anyways on the way home from school. And so, with the sense that the former was better than the latter, an opportunity was arranged for him to spend some time with the two youngest boys. This done, he seized upon the opportunity to keep them. He was staying in the Kingsway Motor Inn near Boundary Road in a small duplex-type cabin suite. The decision had to be made then about what to do, knowing Dad as we did and that he would use them to gain more liberties to the house. We turned to Doug and his friends to secure their return. It was quite an impressive sight, two choppers with leather-clad riders pulled up in front of the half duplex accompanied by Doug in his '64 Merc. Doug went in to initiate the discussions. There was no confrontation and an immediate truce. With just a few door slams, both of the little ones were remitted into the hands of the biker dudes and Doug for safe keeping. They were promptly returned to the house.

Darth returned to his lonely vigil across the street at night, seeking to destabilize us by his presence. Late one night by the light in the oven, with the oven door down, Mom and I prayed that God would remove Dad by taking away his ability to stay in Vancouver. God was in the habit of answering. The next night Dad's car was stolen from the hotel parking lot and driven at breakneck speed through town down 37th Avenue past Klimashes house and into the barricade of police vehicles waiting for it on Main Street. They never did find the driver.

Dad, without wheels, felt the need to withdraw. He returned in four months with a new vehicle, a brown '70 Olds Vista Cruiser station wagon. One afternoon he gained access to the house, grabbed Chris, who was three, and Paul, who was seven, and immediately made a break for the door. Dad took the kids down the back stairs kicking and screaming. Paul made a futile attempt to impede his progress by hanging onto the back railing, an effort that had little effect. Dad threw them both into the waiting vehicle and drove off. As he drove around he encouraged Paul to play with the power windows, believing that would take Paul's mind off of the current situation. But Paul was a little too smart for this. Playing along, he made Dad believe that this was fine, but his master plan was to scream his head off at the first sign of authority. Little did he know that Dad was way ahead of that strategy—he drove around until Chris and Paul fell sleep. So much for Paul's plan. Chris and Paul woke in the dark with Dad driving in a strange city: Portland, Oregon. Actually, driving around strange cities was just like the old days. At daybreak Dad parked the car and told Chris and Paul to stay put or else. Paul knew full well what "or else" could mean, so they stayed put. Chris was very upset the whole time and Paul climbed over the back of the big station wagon and spent hours consoling him. Paul would hold him and point out the window at passing female figures and say, "Look, there is Mommy." This, of course, only served to slow the steady sobbing from Chris. Dad returned and threw in a box of Peak Frean cookies as if he was feeding the dogs. During this time away, unknown to Paul, Dad was in negotiations with Mom and the police over the possible return of his two captives. Later that evening Dad returned to find that the boys had soiled themselves. After all, they had had no bathroom break for two days. Dad affected a partial cleanup using a public washroom at a park. Dad even offered to let Paul drive the car around the parking lot while sitting on his lap, presumably to make him feel better over what was happening. Using the kids as bargaining chips, he negotiated a return to our house. Shortly after he returned with the kids he volunteered to drive Brock, myself, and Allan Wong, a friend of mine, out to a camping trip to a lake hike in the Mamquam river area north of Squamish. I remember the uneasy feeling we had as he drove away from the viewpoint drop-off at the start of the trail. We found out on our return why. He had used this occasion to begin one of his usual one-sided fights with Mom. It started with the usual verbal tirade and ended with him chasing her down the alley behind our house and smashing her in the head with a brick. He dragged the stunned body of our mother back to the house. Fortunately the police were waiting. When he resisted, three officers took him down.

Dad left, never to return. Once released with numerous charges pending, he fled across the line to the US. He was prevented from returning by several court orders against him. We received several hundred six-inch letters from him in San Diego and then ultimately from Tijuana where he lived for the next decades.

Over the years that followed, Doug became a successful trucker, I received an Engineering degree and started an engineering career. Rhonda married a pastor. Brock received his Engineering degree and Master's and developed his professional career. Paul worked for a dairy, eventually buying the route and developing several companies. Chris became the best unpaid comedian in the country and worked with Paul and later for the longest time in the funny farm in Coquitlam. We always hoped he wouldn't lose his ID there.

Miraculously, our faith had survived the horror years. Now reintroduced in the on-fire and faith-filled environment of Fraser View Assembly, it sprang back to life. What God's intervention did to get us out of Smokey Lake through answered prayer showed me that no circumstance, no mater how difficult, is out of God's control. There at Fraser View I learned that He is interested in all the details of our lives, not just in helping us survive. I learned to hear His voice in prayer, to pray in the Spirit and to touch the mind of God in that process. This is not a one-way adventure, however. When you meet God, he has a few suggestions for how you should live. One of those included the fact he wanted me to give up drugs, which at that time I had been doing pretty steadily. With his help that ended. Giving up hard rock took a bit longer.

Doug had a more dramatic experience. While he had been involved in God's miracle to get us out of Smokey Lake, he was in no way inclined to join us at church. "It's full of a bunch of hypocrites," he'd respond when asked if he'd like to go. "I'm not interested in being near a bunch of self-righteous hypocrites." Nothing doing, he wouldn't go—except for one persistent brother, Bob, who if nothing else was stubborn about the fact that Doug would have to come and see what God was doing through the church services. Grudgingly, after repeated refusals to go and as much as to get me off his back as anything, one night he agreed to attend. That night the church was packed. Doug sat behind old Brother Chapman. Mid-service the older gentleman stood up and uncharacteristically gave a word from God. I remember I was in the balcony and when I heard it I knew it was for Doug. He said, "Young man, you have been refusing to serve me. You point to all the hypocrites and problems in the Church. Know that today I am calling you to follow me and serve me. If you do, I will bless you and give you a wife and will bless everything you set your hand to do. But if you will not serve me, I will curse you and will withhold all blessing from you. I'm telling you to decide this day. There will be no other opportunity." Then he turned around and said to Doug, "Young man that word is for you." Brother Chapman had never met Doug or heard of him in his life.

Doug did what any Radloff would do in that situation—he fled the building. I caught him right as he was leaving the back door. He said he didn't have time to talk and was getting out of there as soon as possible. He sat in his car in the parking lot, put the keys in the ignition, started the car and then bowed his head and prayed. That night he gave in to God.

Shortly after he started going to church, Doug met his future wife, Judy, and began to serve God.

Myself, I went on to experience God in my everyday life. I guess I was a bit like Luke Skywalker learning to use his new light sabre—there were a few casualties. Slowly God taught me He lived in a world where principles mattered over expediency, where faith in Him was to be learned and practiced and that He expected me to care for other people as much as myself. In the process He helped steer me through many pitfalls. One example was my first job after graduation. I was in the position that I really needed a job; I had student loans to pay and I was expected to help my family financially. It was understood. Desperately wanting a job, I faithfully fasted and prayed before every on-campus interview that God would help me in the interview process and I'd get a job offer from the firm I was having an interview with.

Now, about that light sabre—if you know a bit about using it you'd probably know it's important to pray more specifically, like "help me get the right job" or "let me be offered only one job—the right one." Unfortunately I needed more training. As a result of this undirected prayer barrage I got my request. All six firms I interviewed with offered me a job, which in turn precipitated prayer number two, for the wisdom now to know which job to take. Even here it was struggle. It came down to two construction firms. I wanted to take the Dillingham job offer, but every time I prayed about it I believed God wanted me to go with Peter Kiewit. I really was annoyed at this because it appeared to me that Dillingham was the big time and Kiewit was small. I was very wrong. Actually, it was much the opposite but I didn't know then. To do what God was directing and yet in hopes of getting the job I wanted I decided I'd go to Kiewit and lay it on the line, give them a big spiel to the effect they'd retract the offer. I went in and asked to see the president of western Canada operations, John Patterson. I said, "I'm a Christian and I don't drink and I don't swear (most of the time)," and on and on. "And if you're going to hire me you have to know that." Of course I was expecting to be thrown out of the office. His answer was a big surprise. "Well, we need more young men of your character in this organization, so we definitely want you to work with us."

"Oh, brother," I thought to myself. "There goes my Dillingham job."

I was to find out a few months later that the job Dillingham had promised to send me to in Iran was cancelled—something about the Shah of Iran being deposed and foreign nationals being expelled from the country with just the clothes on their backs. There, but for the grace of God, I would have been, except that God knew the circumstance and what was in the works all along. He taught me it pays to listen. Most times I do.

*****

It was 1987, seventeen years after my father's departure for Mexico, and except for the very infrequent phone call and 30-page letter from him I wouldn't have known that he existed. Frankly, I didn't care if he did or didn't. Over those years Doug had made a number of requests that we go and see him. My response became like a broken record: "Positively, no. Go yourself, I don't care. Just don't take me with you."

When prisoners get out of jail they don't go back to visit the warden. So it was strange when one evening while praying I had a distinct word from God in my heart that I was to call Doug and tell him that we needed to go down to see Dad. My immediate response was forget it, no way that's not You talking, God. Unfortunately, this persisted and I felt compelled to call Doug the next night and tell him this.

Doug's response was understandably one of surprise. When I told him that we should go see Dad, he said, "Wow, this is incredible!"

My response to that was, "You mean it is incredible that after all these years that I want to go?"

Doug said, "No, it's incredible because Brock called me last night to tell me the same thing." Brock was in Austin, Texas, taking his Master's in Structural Engineering. Brock, being as wary of my Dad as I was, was the last person I would have expected to give Doug that kind of response. This in my mind confirmed the fact that it was indeed God who wanted us to go, though I still did not know why.

We made arrangements to travel to Tijuana, Mexico, to see our dad. Doug and I met in Vancouver and flew by 767 to Los Angeles. Brock drove all across the US to meet up with us at the airport. The night before we crossed the line we slept in San Diego. The next morning we headed out, my father not knowing we were on our way. We approached the border and Brock assured us he would handle it. He was fluent in Spanish and relished the opportunity to show that his efforts of learning the language were about to pay off. On approaching the border guard, from the driver's seat Brock explained quite carefully—in Spanish—where we were going, the purpose of our trip and, it seemed to me, 20 years of history. He seemed not eager to move through the border despite the guard's gesture to move forward. Perhaps real life is just too simple for someone with their Master's. The guard frowned as Brock continued to pontificate in Spanish. Finally, with a great sigh and a brief look upwards, with a concerted effort he stared down at Brock and said, "Fine, fine, Amigo. Just go," in perfect English. As one, Doug and I told him to get moving, and we continued on our way, searching for Avenue Delabeunoes. Brock's knowledge of Spanish did come in handy in finding the correct location. We shortly found ourselves in front of a rambling white house on Avenue Delabeunoes.

We approached the house, Brock first, knocked, and shortly a slight Mexican young man in his late 20's answered the door. When Brock explained—more briefly now—in Spanish that we were the sons of Paul Ray Radloff here to see him, a note of fear came over the young man's face. It was as if he didn't believe it. Several men in the house left immediately from the back of the house when Paul Ray was summoned. He welcomed us into the shabby living room and seated us on several couches. He sat to my immediate right. The exodus of individuals continued. He spoke to us pleasantly as "His Brothers in Christ" —he did not refer to us as his sons.

As the conversation unfolded I sensed a very strong spiritual presence to my right. I am not sure how you sense these things, but it was very pronounced. Powerful and seething. I had the distinct sense that my father was in there somewhere but this was not whom we were discussing things with. As the conversation progressed "it" elaborated greatly on spiritual theories mixed with tales of local experiences. Friends and foes in religious matters.

While the discussion flowed freely it came to a distinct halt when I brought up the subject of the blood of Jesus. I began to explain that only one thing was really needful and that was to be covered with the blood of Jesus in our lives. I didn't look towards him. He began to get agitated. "I might have to throw you people out," he said. "I've done it before." One had the impression he wasn't exaggerating. I heard a distinct guttural sound beside me almost like a gurgling. Dad charged out of the living room and I changed my position to sit across from Doug and Brock who were sitting close to the door.

Dad returned, taking up the seat beside me in my new position, now facing Doug across from me and Brock to my right. Very shortly the conversation, steered by Doug (he is persistent), returned where it had left off. Again I talked about the blood of Jesus, and this time there was a distinct growl. I continued to talk about it and there was a shaking on my side and I only looked at Brock and Doug's faces. Their faces grew quite pale as they stared at the figure beside me.

Finally, my father, in a deep and totally different voice, growled out, "I would gladly die for Jesus." I glanced over to my left and he glanced at me, and what I saw was not the same face I had met at the door 20 minutes ago. His face was contorted, brought forward somehow with a distinct resemblance to a pig's snout, but still that of a man. The face was flushed and bulging red. His eyes lids fluttered eerily as he glared inquisitively at me. I didn't move, and based on years of practice I didn't show fear. No emotion is a good thing at these times. The boys did likewise. "It" became very agitated. Brock spoke up and said he thought it was time to leave. Brock was always good at understatement. Doug was yelling at Dad, telling him that he needed to listen to me about the blood of Jesus. This only served to enrage him further. We decided to go and headed for the front door. Dad followed close behind and then strode off to the back. He returned quickly, almost vaulting across the floor, seemingly not knowing what to do with the three of us. We continued down the sidewalk to Brock's car. Doug decided to bolt back to the house and confront the leering menace on the front step. He shouted at my father—"you leave your family for this, no way, that is not right and not of God." Finally Brock grabbed Doug, but Doug kept yelling as he was dragged towards the car. With Doug safely in the car we drove off. The heavy traffic of Tijuana blurred by in silence.

Once safely across the line in San Diego, each of us still vibrating from what we had just seen, we sat down for supper. No one spoke. Finally Doug broke the silence. He went on to say that maybe we had been too hard on Dad, maybe it was all our fault, maybe we needed to go back there and talk to him so we could sort it all out. This he did for some time, arguing with himself mostly. Eventually Brock paused from his meal, and heretofore completely silent, stated slowly and forcibly, "Doug, Dad is possessed, so shut up and eat your supper." And we all went silent because we knew he was right.

Flying back on the plane to Prince George, I remember the distinct sense that my father was no longer. It was like I was coming from his funeral. It was over in my mind. I hoped it was over in Doug's.

13: The End—Really

IT WAS MARCH 2005. We had just gone down to Vancouver for the weekend. We met Mom that weekend, and as happens more often than not when you drop in to Mom's, my brother Brock is apt to drop by. He dropped by that weekend too.

"How would I get hold of Dad if I wanted to?" he asked.

"Just get in touch with Doug," I said. Doug had made an effort to stay in touch with Dad by mail and by phone ever since our encounter with him 18 years earlier. We knew about this, but Doug mostly kept this contact with Dad to himself.

"He mentioned he was in touch with Dad and he thought he was getting better," I added. "Give him a call and you might get his phone number from Doug, if he has one."

I left it at that, though I was curious why he would be so interested in getting in touch with Dad after all these years. If I was curious I didn't ask. Brock usually had a good reason for his actions. I figured he could deal with it himself. Returning home from Vancouver I got a call from Doug. It was Dad, he said. "He's been out of touch with me for a long time."

"How long?" I asked.

"About two months."

I thought that wasn't much, all things considered, but Doug felt uneasy about it. He had some sense that something was wrong.

"Well, Brock was talking to me about how to get ahold of Dad," I said. "Has he called you?"

"No," Doug said. He indicated he would follow up with some more calls to see if Dad could be reached. Maybe he'd contact the Canadian Embassy to see if they had heard anything. Maybe Dad was dead or something.

The next day Doug was on the line again.

"The Canadian Consulate called looking for us," he said. "They had a call from the Tijuana office. Dad's in a clinic in Tijuana in critical condition. He's been on the street, kicked out of his residence, for two months. The clinic and the boarding house he was from both wanted to be paid." He told me Brock had called and he relayed this to Brock.

Brock, Doug and I compared notes over several phone calls and resolved that we had to do something. We couldn't just leave him there on the streets to die. That something might be putting him in a hospital there, or one here in Canada. If his condition wasn't life-threatening, "something" could mean just getting him well enough to get him back into a residence down there.

The one thing we agreed on was he couldn't come back to live anywhere near Mom.

We set up a plan. Brock would take a station wagon down from his place in Vancouver to Tijuana in case we had to bring him back. Doug would fly down to LA where Brock would pick him up on his way to Tijuana. We would split the costs three ways. We didn't think Brock should go down alone. Doug shared with us that the Lord had given him a scripture, Psalm 71 v.9 which states: "Do not forsake me when I am old and grey."

Brock set out for Mexico with a Taurus wagon and drove through the night. Picking up Doug in LA, they proceeded quickly to San Diego and then on to Tijuana. The sight of Dad in the clinic was an object lesson in what not to do with your life, Brock said later. He was a mess: bruised and emaciated, matted hair, laying in the filthy conditions of the clinic. Upon sight of Brock and Doug he brightened up some. They asked him what he wanted to do. "Do you want to stay here or go with us?" they asked.

"I'm better off with you two than with these guys," he said. He wanted to go back to Canada. At that moment someone bumped the bed in which he was laying. Instantly the rage inside him was awakened and he went after the person verbally with all he had.

"Shut up, Dad," Doug said.

The response was low and guttural, a different voice.

"What are you going to do about it?" he glowered back, staring Doug in the face. They knew Dad was not changed.

Doug and Brock left to think this one through. To bring him back in this physical and spiritual condition would be dangerous. After they conferred with the consulate coordinator in her office she left. There, sitting on her desk, was a ceremonial Bible used for swearing statements. Unknown to Doug, in it was inserted a small ragged piece of paper for a bookmark. Doug leaned over, took the Bible and it opened directly to the bookmark page. The paper rested directly across the page from Psalm 71 v.9: "Do not forsake me when I am old and grey."

They looked at each other and knew that, despite the challenge, they needed to take Dad out of there.

Just to make sure, Brock took the Bible and shook it upside down, just checking to make sure there were no other clues or bookmarks present. Maybe there would be a sign that they shouldn't do it. Nothing else fell out. Well, he did try.

They made arrangements to have Dad transferred from the clinic to their care. This included paying the clinic's outstanding bill, additional medication for the trip and new clothes for Dad to replace the fetid, urine-soaked ones he had with him. The consulate arranged for an emergency visa. Armed with this, they accompanied the ambulance to the Mexican border where Dad was transferred to the Taurus wagon. He was placed on the mattress and they were off.

The patient in the back had been hard for the ambulance attendants to handle. He would be equally hard to handle for the two of them. Eighty years old, emaciated, beat up and suffering a swollen bladder from cancer, he was still as much as the two could handle.

He never slept. All through the night he scratched and clawed at the back of the station wagon, pulling at the light and wires leading to the light, at the door handles and the carpet. When Doug would nod off from sheer exhaustion, Dad's hand would reach over and grab his head, waking him from his rest. Again and again he would slap and scratch at them in the front and wreak havoc on the back of the car. They resorted to strapping him down, but still he persisted. Tireless. He would at times be lucid, speaking to them for moments on topics about anything they could distract him with. Just as quickly he would be enveloped by the fearful personality that would threaten and harass them. They drove on, through Nevada, Utah and on to Montana.

Jane and I prayed as they drove. The last we heard of them they had just crossed into Utah from Arizona. On that phone call I was speaking to Doug and there was a sudden shout, "Look out! Stop! Watch out! Stay on the road!" and then the phone went dead. I found out later Dad had pulled the wiring out of the roof and had tried to open one of the rear doors. Doug had dropped the phone to intervene and a fight had ensued. They called minutes later to say they were alright.

The next morning Jane and I returned home for lunch and to pray.

"Where do you think they are?" she asked, pulling a map of western Canada and the US out for reference. Jane is always organized.

Looking over the map, I said, "Right there," pointing at Butte, Montana.

"I think they're right there in Butte, Montana," I said.

On the way in to work after lunch we got the call.

"Hi, it's Brock. We're down here still in the US," he said, haltingly. "We're beside the road and . . . and Dad's dead."

After some silence I asked where they were.

"We're in Butte, Montana," he said, his voice still a bit shaky. After some discussion it was agreed they would bring Dad's body to the nearest hospital. We thought that would be the best thing to do. I mean, what else could you do? The border situation was a lot tighter after 9/11, so you could be sure there would be trouble if you got caught crossing with a dead person.

The decision turned out to be the right one. After examination by the local coroner and some consultation with the local sheriff, it was concluded by the authorities that Brock and Doug's stories made sense. The Sheriff admonished them both for their efforts to save Dad. Based on the data they had, it was a Herculean effort.

Later, Doug and Brock related what had happened in the hours before Dad's death. During the previous 18 hours, they had wrestled and fought with this thing in the back of the station wagon. In southern Montana on a lonely stretch of road, Doug had finally had enough. Full of righteous indignation, he turned to the upstretched twin claws of hands once again reaching to grab the light, and shouted, "I command you, spirit, to loose this man and leave him now forever!"

There was a silence and the hands slowly went down, finally resting by his sides. There was a brief sigh and Dad went to sleep for the first time since leaving Mexico. The only sound other than the hum of the tires on the endless pavement was Dad's heavy breathing—deep, restful breaths, as finally for the first time in many days the tortured soul in the back slept.

He passed away in his sleep 30 minutes later, free from the influence of the evil spirit that tormented him many years.

He rested now in the back seat, in a car between destinations, not unlike our own experiences as kids. He waited now for his sons to decide what to do, and not the other way around.

14: The Benz

THERE WAS A MEMORIAL SERVICE scheduled for Dad in Star City, Saskatchewan. The Mercedes 500S was great to travel in. It was roomy enough for Doug, Judy, myself and Jane, plus luggage. We picked up Brock at the Saskatoon airport and added him and associated luggage to the load. We headed to Star City at high speed, listening to Johnny Cash. It felt a bit strange to be back in Saskatchewan after all these years. Maybe it was the car that didn't fit; maybe it was that we actually listened to Johnny Cash. All this didn't seem to matter, though, when we reached the turnoff to Star City.

There, the inconspicuous entrance loomed up on our left. A small sign pointed to our destination. The car slowed, and with all the guttural power of our grandfather's old Mercury, the car turned onto the narrow secondary road that leads to the town site, on down to the second left into town where the old Royalite gas station once stood. The big poplar where we had impaled the once new Dodge was gone. So was the gas station. But the memory was there, big as ever.

No crashes today, though—we're pretty much civilized now. The main street is all but vacant; one or two cars saddle up against the empty sidewalks. Everything is silent and surreal. The old Serve U store still stands, still armoured in the pressed tin brick look-alike of the '50s. The old red brick post office, the elevators and houses all stand much as they were years ago, some with new owners and some with no owners. One of them serves for TV and small appliance repair. Most of the stores are empty. It's a far cry from the bustling town on a Friday night in the '50s.

The memorial service was conducted in the Pentecostal church where we as a family had attended many years before. Those were the happy years, I'm told. Many who remembered Dad attended—family and friends. They say a statesman is a politician who's been dead for ten years. So it was with Dad. The eulogy said all the right things about the good Paul Rae of years ago. For the most part, no one knew the father we had come to know: "THE" Paul Rae as some would call him. But that's not what mattered now. All that mattered is that it came to an end.

I returned to the car for one important item, the cremated remains of Dad which I was informed were in the trunk. Lifting the trunk, there they were. A small five-inch-by-five-inch plastic box with a label "Paul Rae Radloff 1925—2005," it read. I recall clearly the thought: "So here in this plastic box are the remains of all the violence and fear and horrible memories of my life. He can't hurt me now. Of that I'm sure."

I closed the trunk, box in hand, and walked into the moaning prairie wind.

15: Epilogue

I'M NOT SURE HOW this all works out on a theological basis: as all things must, I suppose. It's obvious God was gracious and saved us in the nick of time (some would say at the appointed time) from an eminent madman. And rather than appearing as a late night news item where people could shake their heads wondering at the sad story of a domestic situation gone far wrong, as a result of God's grace we live, go on and prosper. A good thing.

And what of the volcanic creature of rage and hurt that had "mopped the floor" with so many during his lifetime? Strong to the end, beyond belief. Defiant and cunningly vociferous. Was that the real man? I got the sense the real man was far below, curled up and rarely let out. Was God's grace sufficient for him, too? Did God intervene long enough to separate the two and allow the inner man to die in peace, to be joined with the one who knows all things, sees all things, and though circumstances scream otherwise, never lets matters reach beyond His restoring grace—not even for such a one as this?

I think so. Some day I'll know.

Printed in the United States
102798LV00001B/103-174/P

9 781897 373224